FATHER MARQUETTE

GREAT MEN OF MICHIGAN
EDITED BY C. WARREN VANDER HILL

FATHER MARQUETTE

by

RAPHAEL N. HAMILTON, S.J.

WILLIAM B. EERDMANS/PUBLISHER

Dedicated
to
James C. Windham,
National Chairman,
The Father Marquette
Tercentenary Commission
1968-1973
Appointed by
Lyndon B. Johnson

PREFACE

This biography of Father Jacques Marquette was written with the hope of bringing into focus the life of a character whose pioneering accomplishments in the seventeenth century are rather well known. Because they were so exciting, they have pushed the man aside and left his image somewhat indistinct. For my purpose the "why" and the "how" of what he did are more important than the "what." The latter will not be neglected, and a bibliographical essay has been included in which the reader may find materials that delve more deeply into Father Marquette's life. My effort in the present book has been to pass on to others what I have learned about Father Marquette by mature deliberation on the original manuscripts concerning him. These manuscripts come from Canada's Collège Sainte-Marie in Montreal and the Archives de la Province in Quebec, from Paris's Bibliothèque Nationale and Archives Nationales, from Chantilly's Jesuit Archives de la Province de France, from Rome's Archivum Romanum Societatis Jesu, from special collections in Washington at the Congressional Library, from New York's Public Library, and from Chicago's Newberry Library and the Chicago Historical Society.

The custodians of all the depositories mentioned have been very helpful. To them I express my thanks. Likewise, I am grateful to the Provincial of the Jesuit Province of Wisconsin, Very Reverend Joseph Sheehan, who gave me permission to publish, to one of my teaching colleagues, Father Stephen J. Rueve, who gave me good advice after carefully reading the manuscript, and to Miss Mildred M. Holly, who typed the pages for the printer. Finally, a most sincere "thank you" to my editor, whose generous cooperation has done much to improve this book.

Raphael N. Hamilton

Milwaukee, Wisconsin

CONTENTS

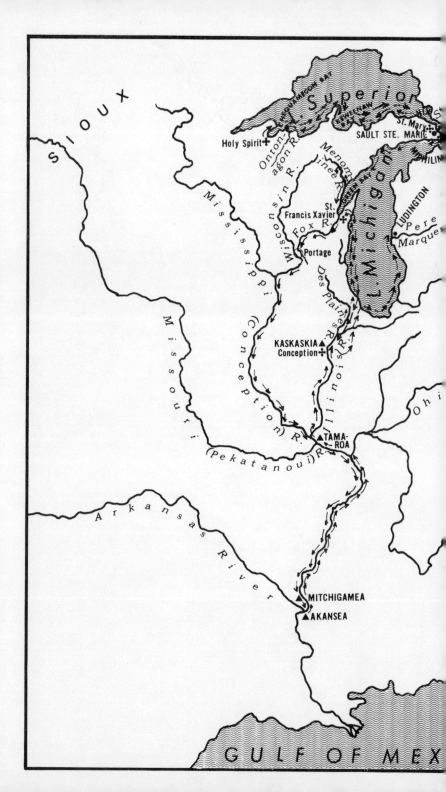

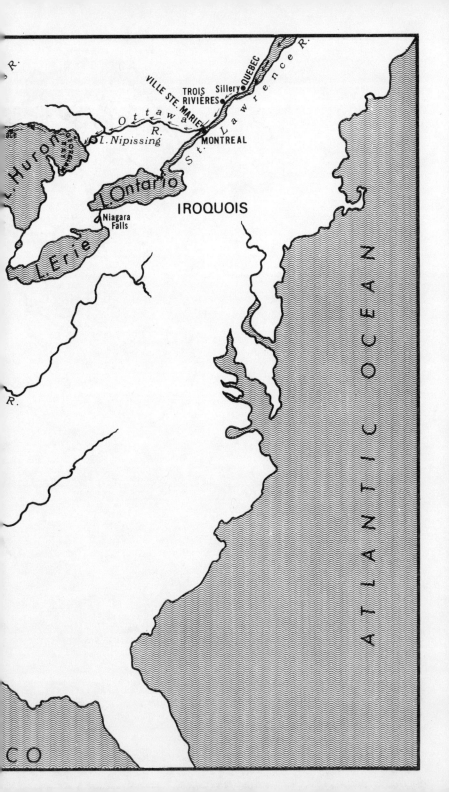

INTRODUCTION

The continents of the Western Hemisphere were discovered by Europeans at one of the high tides of their cultural development. This era is known in history as the Renaissance. New types of art and architecture, advances in medicine and other sciences, geniuses like Ghiberti, Bramante, Michelangelo, and Da Vinci were to make the period one of the most important in the story of mankind. Columbus, returning from his first trip, shocked this advanced society by his account of the cultural conditions he had come upon among the people at the end of his westward voyage. The Moorish principality of Granada, with its marvelous palace of the Alhambra, had been won by Ferdinand and Isabella just before they commissioned the exploration of the Atlantic. They had expected a sort of culture similar to Granada's in India. Instead, their Admiral told them that he had found an unbroken wilderness with only an occasional village inhabited by primitive people, who knew not the use of such simple things as iron tools to cut building stones or wheels to transport them.

When the Renaissance man fully realized that it was not Marco Polo's Orient, but a new world which formed the western shore of the Atlantic Ocean, the human instinct for land ownership began to pull in that direction. Since Europe was divided among kings and nobles, he could not satisfy his land hunger here. But over there, a mere fraction of the number of men which made up the European population was lost in a domain so extensive that it could never be completely occupied by these aborigines. Like a contagious fever, the wish to be off for a new home spread from one country to another. The authorities who were responsible for opening the way to such possessions were faced with a problem. There were vacant acres aplenty in the West, but how could they justify taking them away from the primitive persons who had come there first? They turned to their philosophers to find a reasonable medium of exchange by which this uninhabited patrimony might be bought. The answer of the thinkers was that offering money to the natives for their heritage was out of the question, because coins without a market were valueless. However, considering the condition of these people, it seemed one could adequately repay them for the vacant territory by taking it in exchange for the civilizing elements of Christian culture. Agriculture, science, health, comfort, beauty, a knowledge of the true God were blessings which had immediate

11

value for the Indians. The statesmen were satisfied. They wrote into the patents of colonizers a demand for them to dispense these things for what property they took.

When France became a colonizing country, it adopted the civilization-for-empire formula. By then it was known that not all natives favored the way this theory had often been put into practice. The part of it which had succeeded best was the work of the missionaries, who brought the Indians some solace from their superstitious fears. Thus, invariably, French priests accompanied French explorers and colonizers. Hundreds of them participated in spreading the gospel during the French regime in North America. Among these, Father Jacques Marquette is one of the best known because of his part in the discovery of the Mississippi River. The whole of mid-America has heard about him, has befriended him, has perpetuated his name by attaching it to institutions and cities. But, perhaps, the state of Michigan has a special claim to him, since within its boundaries he did most of his work for the Indians. The present book hopes to set forth, more clearly than ever before, the kind of man Marquette was while he lived there. The people who live in Michigan now will thus appreciate why he deserves to be numbered among their great men.

CHAPTER 1:

SCHOOL DAYS

It has stood there for nobody knows how long: the rock of Laon. It is sizeable enough to support a town within a bracelet of cut-stone walls. The town is large enough to have had as many parishes as there are fingers on a hand, perhaps a dozen oratories besides, and over them all a proud cathedral. The rock of Laon is high enough to have required many oxen to haul each lumbering cartload of masonry, brought from the plain to the summit, when the mother church was being built in 1155. The builders perpetuated the cooperation of these patient beasts by carving their effigies where they still look down from the twin towers flanking the oriel on the structure's western front.

Why should this great rock be placed just there on the savanna of the duchy of Champagne, now the department of Aisne, in France? The site is a strategic one. From it roads stretch northward across the Low Countries to the cold waters which separate the land of the Angles from the Norseman's fiords. Eastward, the thoroughfares spread out through the vineyards of the Rhine to the forests of the Danube, home of the Teuton-Germanies. Caesar's legions trod those roads when they went out to fight the Belgae and the Britons. Charlemagne led his troops over them when he brought the continent of Europe into the Holy Roman Empire. The Creator seems to have placed the rock where it is to be a fortress guarding "La Belle France," a sally port when "La Patrie" sent forth its sons to conquest. French kings were not slow to appreciate this. Four of them held their court on its summit.

Clovis was the first king of France. A fifth-century pagan Frank by birth, he might have been just another barbaric invader like the many who came into Europe after A.D. 410, when the Roman Empire began to fall apart. St. Remy, born at Laon and bishop of Reims, baptized him at a crisis in his career. Then he blessed his campaign, which went on to subdue Visigothic chiefs and Roman legates until Clovis set up his court in Paris, with the Pyrenees for the sourthern boundary of his realm. Remy's nephew became Laon's

13

first bishop. After the town's cathedral was erected, three of its prelates were called to Rome to be made popes—Urban IV, Nicholas III, and Clement VI.

It was no wonder that Laonians taught their children to love the king and pope. In the exciting period of the Renaissance, many a starry-eyed boy of Laon had shed his blood on the old-world battle fields of his monarch or breathed out his soul on the new-world mission fields of his pontiff. The tradition of the Laonians was built on one of the most mysterious yet also one of the truest elements of human nature: love is happiest when it gives to the loved one without counting the cost, and supremely happy when the gift is the entire abandonment of one's self.

The people of Laon are justly proud of their heritage, but it is to a man born there on June 1, 1637, who had little to do with the things of its history, that they have raised a monument that they cherish most. This man was Jacques Marquette. His father and mother combined all the best traditions of the city lore. Nicholas Marquette traced his ancestry back through a line of warriors. He himself was counselor of the municipality. He was known at court; he had taken the side of King Henry IV. His wife, Rose De La Salle, who presided over the big house in the parish of St. Pierre le Viel where she gave birth to Jacques, came from a pious family in Reims one of whose descendants, St. John-Baptist De La Salle, born 1651, founded the Brothers of the Christian Schools. In this pleasant home, with two sisters and three brothers, Jacques spent the happy years of innocence.

No one bothered to trace the progress of the boy's age and growth. Only one incident before his ninth birthday can be established with any certainty. When Jacques was six years old, there was a great pilgrimage to the shrine of Liesse, eight miles away, to pray for the recovery of King Louis XIII. Almost all of the Laonians went. Jacques's father and mother, by reason of the former's office, must surely have gone with the crowd, and a healthy six-year-old was probably taken along.

Why save Louis XIII? Because France was at war again, and, if he died, it would leave the command of the French army to a baby son. The cause of the Thirty Years' War went back to Speyer in 1529, when rumblings of national discontent among the Germans had erupted. An Augustinian monk, summoned before the high court of the realm because of strange religious teachings, lodged a protest at which the volcano exploded. The blast split the German church. To the north, all became Lutherans, named after the monk, or Protestants, named after the protest. The south, at the Diet of Augsburg (1555), was told by the emperor to follow the belief of each prince; and, at the ecumenical council of Trent, all were told by the Pope to shun the teaching of Luther or be anathema. By 1618, the struggle for power between the two factions had become the Thirty Years' War (1618-1648).

After twenty years of fighting, France entered the war. Cardinal Richelieu, Louis XIII's minister, who had brought the power of the French king to a height never before dreamed of in the land, saw his chance to make France pre-eminent in Europe. His plan was to humiliate the Catholic Emperor of Germany so that the Holy Roman Empire would lose the respect of nations, and his monarch would win their fear. The scheme was working. For five years victorious armies had marched east along the roads which stretched from the base of the rock of Laon. Then, in 1643, Louis became sick. Despite the pilgrimage to Liesse, he died the same year. His young son became Louis XIV at the age of five. Nor did Richelieu live to see the final success of his plans. He led his king into eternity. However, a man whom he had trained, Cardinal Jules Mazarin, kept the armies marching until the German empire collapsed in 1648 and, at Westphalia, fell weak and bleeding into the arms of its foe.

The Marquettes were soldiers by tradition. With this background, Jacques seemed fated to grow into a uniform, to buckle on a sword, and to follow the eastward road toward the rising sun of France and war. He might have done just that had it not been for Monsignor Brichanteau, the bishop of Laon. He knew the boy in 1646: perhaps Jacques sang in the cathedral choir, perhaps he served as acolyte there, and perhaps his father entertained the prelate in the large house in the parish St. Pierre le Viel. At any rate, the bishop saw to it that Jacques was sent to the Jesuit university at Reims at the age of nine, which seems incredible today. This particular school was probably chosen because the boy's mother had relatives there. Any seventeenth-century university admitted students as soon as they knew the rudiments of Latin. This much Jacques had been taught by a priest relative. Young Marquette was to end his studies for the bachelor's degree in 1654, just after his seventeenth birthday. The fine old building where he spent those eight years still stands today. Now it is the General Hospital of Reims.

Bonfires of the French Revolution (1789) consumed the archives of Marquette's alma mater; therefore, his undergraduate life can only be pictured by reference to the general pattern of seventeenth-century Jesuit education. The humanities—Greek and Latin, history, poetry, oratory, philosophy, and Christian theology—were the high points of the curriculum. Extracurricular activities included intra-mural sports, speech contests, stage performances, and membership in the sodality. A Jesuit who knew Marquette tells of the boy's fascination with the Blessed Virgin, which came from this student society aimed at honoring her. During the meetings, it was customary to recite the "little office," patterned on the longer priestly breviary but restricted to scriptural verses and prayers about the Mother of God. Jacques was so captivated by her charm that he

15

carried this practice over into his daily routine; and, in the Laonian tradition, he determined to do something difficult to show his love. At the age of nine, in his first year at college, he began fasting in her honor on Saturdays.[1] His earnestness in a known incident of school life provides some evidence for believing that he participated in all of the school's offerings with equal zest.

It is certain that at Reims Marquette made up his mind what he would do with his life. Three years before he came here, Martin De Lyonne was the first local Jesuit to go to Canada. While preparing for ordination, Father Peter Beschefer, a faculty member at Reims, had followed the course in theology with him. These incentives for an extraordinary interest in the North American missions were fresh when Marquette came to the college. He was in his fourth year and had just reached adolescence, that awesome period of youthful idealism, when he learned that two of Father De Lyonne's companions had met sudden death. Father Jean De Brebeuf and Father Gabriel De Lalemant had been executed at the stake by the Iroquois Indians. The professor who told the boys of their torture went on to say that the Hurons, among whom the missionaries worked and who had seen the martyrdom, wonderingly told of the martyrs' joy in dying. How, asked young Marquette, could anyone show joy at such a time? De Brebeuf and De Lalemant loved God so much that they were made happy by giving him the best thing they had—their lives. To the boy steeped in the Laonian traditions, this made sense. During the four remaining years of his studies, the explanation for the missionaries' happiness must have had some influence on Marquette when he pondered his own career. It seemed to him that he must give all to God to be happy. He decided that he would be a Jesuit missionary, and he chose the saint of the missions, Francis Xavier, for his patron.

On vacation a few years later, Jacques was a bit surprised by what he saw in the full-length pier glass before him. At college there were few mirrors, and they were tiny things. Tonight he was in his father's house. He had just finished his junior year at the university and was in Laon for vacation. The officers at the citadel near the bishop's palace had invited him to a ball to celebrate the success of the king's troops in handling a revolt known in French history as the *Fronde*. The reflection Jacques saw revealed the result of a consistent program of collegiate sports that for seven years had paralleled his studies at Reims. This program had developed the nine-year-old child into an athletic man almost full-grown. His open face was good-natured, with something about the curve of the jaw, the depth of the eyes, and the height of the forehead that added a pleasing earnestness to his expression. His chest was deep, his hips were small, his legs were straight, his arms were muscular. His buff-colored satin suit fit him well. The brass knuckles at his knees and on his pumps caught the light warmly. The lace at his throat and wrists set off, by contrast, a strong neck and hands.[2] He had not realized how much he had changed. A man who looked like that ought to be able to take care of himself.

With abundant greenery and festoons of flowers, the *salle d'armes* had been changed into a ballroom for the night. Here a tireless orchestra accompanied the swirls and curtsies of the couples intent upon the intricacies of the quadrille and minuet. A nearby corner of the parade ground, trellised off from the rest, had become a labyrinth where little tables were sheltered in the alcoves between potted shrubs and vines. Here servants offered champagne and heady punch for the refreshment of fatigued dancers. Candles everywhere winked back at the stars above.

The young man in the buff-colored suit proved popular. He was a graceful dancer and a good conversationalist. Many of the young ladies had been his childhood friends. He realized that the past seven years had affected them as much as himself. They too had matured: they wore fashionable party dresses and jewelry, and some powdered their hair and placed a tiny black patch on their cheek to enhance the clarity of their complexion. They were fair to look on. They seemed glad to be his partners, whether he was leading them over the dance floor or sitting with them at the refreshment table. It was almost dawn when Jacques came home. As he tumbled into bed, he was happy with the pleasure of having received all these delightful things. Just as he was dozing off, a thought came to his mind which made him sit bolt upright. Was it wrong for him, who had hoped to be a Jesuit, to be happy like this? From somewhere in his head an answer took shape: personal happiness is not wrong; it is wrong to imagine that the person who has everything is happy. He lay down and slept peacefully.

In a few days the young Laonian was back at college devoting himself to the final study of philosophy, and each day he became more convinced of the logic which had led him to the choice of his vocation. Almost as soon as he had received his A.B., he set out for the novitiate. It was October, 1654.

CHAPTER 2:

JESUIT TRAINING

Not only enthusiasm, but care and worry were fellow passengers with young Marquette while the coach bearing him to the Jesuit house at Nancy rattled along the monotonous road. They were unwelcome companions. They kept telling him that the step he was taking was very different from his previous trips to school. On those occasions he had money to spend and thoughts of vacation to come. Now he was voluntarily abandoning these things.

At the journey's end, he received a kindly welcome from his novice master. He was shown around the building, to his quarters, and naturally to the chapel. But now, as he knelt alone before the silent altar, he knew he did not want to turn back. To be a Jesuit was what he wanted above all because—and youthful enthusiasm now had the last word—he, Jacques Marquette, loved God and wanted to give him his life. One gives such a gift by doing the will of the loved one. The happiness of loving became his possession once more. A great calm settled on his soul as he resigned himself to the will of the Lord whose presence in the tabernacle became so real. He was just four months and three days past his seventeenth birthday.

In 1656, at the end of his time of probation, Marquette gladly confirmed the resolution to follow his vocation by taking the vows which made him a member of the Society of Jesus. At the same time that he did so, the young French king had reached his eighteenth year with smug faith in a destiny which would stamp his name, Louis XIV of France, on the period of world history in which he lived. One year younger than Marquette, his education had not been in a university but in the court and *Parlement* of Paris, under the strict tutelage of the wily diplomat and politician, Mazarin. The Bourbon prince was the complete antithesis of the young man from Laon. When Marquette took a vow to obey God in his superiors, Louis swore to be a divine-right monarch with unlimited dominion.

While Marquette was a novice, his temperament was evaluated by his superior as combining a delight in spiritual values, which separated him from earthlings, and a generosity toward the wants of the needy, which indicated the zeal of an apostle. This was good material to work with in the formation of a priest, and the training of a Jesuit was well planned for such formation. Loyola had written an inspired *Constitution* for his order. One part of it set forth the method of making a boy into a dedicated member of the Company of Jesus. Wisely, both in training and in the field, he insisted on a combination of contemplation and action. Early in the years of preparation he made the "first experiment," as he called it. This was a retreat of thirty days. For a month an expert guided the novices in meditating on Christ, the model of all Jesuits, according to the method set forth by Ignatius Loyola during his own conversion and set down in his book, *The Spiritual Exercises.* The place where this was done was to be in quiet surroundings, separated from the hurly-burly of the world. The youths engaged in this work were to keep silence, only to be broken during conferences with the director. When the experiment ended, the men were prepared to take advantage of the daily hour of contemplation prescribed by the rule of their life. This rule also set aside a fifteen-minute examination of conscience, noon and night, to see how things were going, and the yearly repetition of the retreat, reduced to eight days.

After the Council of Trent (1563) had condensed the teaching of Catholic dogma into a catechism of question and answer, novices were sent out to teach these truths to the children of the neighborhood and thus to become acquainted with the scope and content of theology. Other "experiments" included caring for the chores of the house where the Jesuits lived, working in the hospitals, and going on pilgrimages, begging their food along the way. In addition to these activities, the common recreations at some simple villa on the outskirts of town afforded young Jesuits a weekly opportunity to match team against team in games which encouraged good sportsmanship. Another part of their training consisted of teaching the lower classes in colleges of their order, where they became responsible for showing the youngsters the path they should follow. This had been Marquette's life until 1665, when he was assigned to the immediate preparation for the priesthood by a complete course of theology at the University of Pont-à-Mousson.

The Feast of St. Joseph, March 19, is always celebrated with some special observance in the Society of Jesus. In 1665, when Marquette entered the recreation room of the scholastics, he found them looking over the announcement of their appointments for the following school year. The list, sent out from the provincial's residence on that day, was always a source of good-natured banter among the men concerned. If one's appointment was changed, it was because the administration did not appreciate him. If a lower class fell to the lot of another, he must have been lacking in ability to cope with the higher scholarship. Marquette found his name among those who were to begin preparation for the priesthood. This was different. As soon as he could, he slipped away and sought his room. He had always believed that he was to be a missionary. Shortly after becoming a Jesuit, he had written the general superior in Rome, expressing his belief. He had been told that he was too young then. Now he was twenty-eight. His experiments were finished. He sharpened his quill pen, dipped it into the inkwell on his desk, and began a letter to Father Oliva, head of the Jesuit Order at that time.

This letter of March 19, 1665, tells of the letter he had sent on the same subject years before and why he had not been allowed to go abroad. Now he wished to follow the steps of St. Francis Xavier, his patron, and to do so as quickly as possible. He reminded the general of ways he might pursue which would not delay the fulfillment of his wish. He knew that there was a short course of theology that Ignatius had introduced for priests not destined to dispute about speculative dogmas of religion. He wondered if perhaps he could be placed in this course, and perhaps even in a theologate located in the mission country itself. Such a request would exclude him from becoming a "professed father," as those who completed the long course were called. Professed fathers alone shaped the policies of the order. He did not wish to shape policies; he wished to be shaping souls, and to be about it soon. He knew vaguely that the Jesuits had seminaries in India and Canada. He suggested being sent to one of these places immediately. It seemed perfectly logical to him to be where he might learn the language and customs of the aborigines at the same time that he studied dogma. He paused. Another possibility presented itself. His Jesuit training had fulfilled all the requirements for ordination demanded by the recent Council of Trent, with the exception of an examination in moral theology. Would Father General let him be ordained without studying any more of the speculative branches, since he had been working privately on this practical one?

There was nothing extraordinary in ordaining a seventeenth-century Jesuit without formal courses in speculative theology. In 1582, after Trent, Pope Gregory XIII had granted all bishops general permission to raise to the priesthood any member of the Jesuit Order who might be presented for ordination by his provincial. Marquette added to his letter a suggestion that this dispensation was applicable in his case. He penned a final sentence telling the general that above all he wished to be a good son of the Society, asking him to pray for his becoming such.[1]

Some students of Marquette's life have interpreted his letter of March 19, 1665, as a sly indication of his lack of interest in intellectual matters. This is not a legitimate deduction concerning a young man who had taught progressively lower and more advanced classes until, in the year in which he addressed General Oliva, he was teaching "Humanities," the equivalent of a college course in present-day curricula. Only when exceptional talent was recognized were young Jesuits who had not finished all their own studies permitted to assume such a scholastic chair. The exception was probably made in Marquette's favor because he was one of the few unordained mentors who had made time for extra self-instruction during his regency and, by so doing, had acquired a master's degree.

Through the final days of his teaching and while correcting the exams, Jacques found himself occasionally counting the days since he had written his letter. Surely, he thought there had been time enough for a reply to come; but he received no answer. The scholastics destined for theology were free from their books for a couple of weeks. Exercise to keep the mind wholesome in a healthy body was part of Ignatian discipline. Jacques had just been asked to make a foursome for tennis. He hurried to his room to make ready; and there was the letter on his desk. He broke the seal and read: "Your letter of March 19, from which I learn that you burn with an ardent desire to go on the foreign missions was most welcome." He skipped on. "I am writing Father Provincial to ascertain his judgement." What did that mean? He read the letter carefully a second time. There was no indication of approval for his request. If the provincial's reply went back to Rome and was answered in as leisurely a manner as his own letter had been, he would be halfway through the first year of study for ordination before any decision could be made. In the winter there was no chance to go to the foreign missions; boats did not sail. If he spent a full year in the long course . . . ! His thoughts were interrupted by his companions, all ready for the game. He hurried to join them, but he did not play as well as usual. Why was he hitting the ball so hard? Why did the back line seem to shrink up close to the net? "Do what you're doing," another Jesuit aphorism popped into his head. Do what you are doing applied to the letter, too. By the time the game was over, he had made up his mind. He would leave the mission career to providence. Life was a game which did not depend entirely on the player's effort. There was a God who shaped men's destinies. When he had entered the society, he had freely chosen to obey superiors, because he believed in this. Since he believed this, it was only immaturity which would suggest opposition to a decision of his highest superior. He had not become a Jesuit to have his feelings pampered. An intellectual evaluation of his purpose for living had conditioned the free act of his will. Whether or not he won the tennis game that afternoon, he came a long way toward winning the one thing worthwhile in life. Thereafter, the passing joys and sorrows of the world in which he lived could not deeply disturb his peace of soul, because he had realized so clearly their insignificance in comparison to the everlasting destiny which was to be his. Values without decisions are empty, but decisions without values are blind.

The school year of 1665 at the University of Pont-à-Mousson began with Marquette enrolled among the "Reviewers." Men in this class prepared for a comprehensive examination in philosophy. If they passed it, they were destined to take the long course in theology, which lasted from four to six years. It usually led to a chair of theology in a college, a pulpit in a fashionable church, or a confessional where a sophisticated society sought solace. Rarely did the professed of the Company of Jesus go to work among the aborigines in foreign lands. Just after the school year began, Marquette's superior had occasion to assess his temperament. He found him excelling in thoughtfulness for others, with an exceptional ability to get along with them in pleasant association. From this it is clear that no one suspected the sacrifice Marquette had just made.

CHAPTER 3:

MISSION ASSIGNMENT

Louis XIV, who had sworn his oath when Marquette took his vows, had been comfortably successful in the accomplishment of what he had set himself to do. Kings had to love selected princesses rather than girls they loved. Maria Theresa, Infanta of Spain, only daughter of King Philip IV and sister of the Spanish monarch's only son, became Louis's wife. In 1665, Philip's death brought a mentally retarded Charles II to the Spanish throne. He never married, and this opened tremendous political possibilities for France. The Iberian peninsula, the whole of South America, some of North America, the Pacific, and the Philippines beyond—lands extending halfway around the world—might come to France, if Louis could persuade the Spaniards to stand by the natural right of his wife and place her on the throne. Louis XIV, in fact, did live to see his grandson crowned king of Spain.

His English cousin, Charles Stuart, who had fled to his court when the Puritan revolution broke out, had been restored to the British throne in 1660. But he and his brother James were supported by Louis. After a few years, he would assure their independence from their nation of shopkeepers. He pensioned them in return for their promise to come into the Catholic Church and stay out of the Dutch War. In 1672, he was struggling to expand the boundaries of France to the Rhine River. And, at the same time, he re-emphasized a latent tradition of Gallican liberty in the French Church that would have made him a sort of pope in the confines of his empire.

In 1663, in preparation for world imperialism, Louis had organized the administration of the French colonies. The French East India Company was incorporated with exclusive trade rights in the Orient. The West India Company received a similar charter for the Western Hemisphere. Supposedly, these were to be stock companies; but the king had them both under his control by 1665. To open the way for successful trade, nothing could be better than promotion of peaceful infiltration, east and west, by means of the Christian missions. The establishment of his companies was concomitant with his dedication of a new congregation to be known as "Priests of the Foreign Missions." He dispatched three bishops from the group to the East. To the West he sent Jean Baptiste Talon,

Alexandre De Prouville, the Marquis De Tracy. Soldiers were also sent to crush the troublesome Iroquois in the hope that, once they were under control, the Jesuit missions could care for the rest. So successful was the latter strategy that, as Marquette was beginning his theological training, news came of a Jesuit penetration of remote new lands at the far western end of Lake Superior, where nations with 100,000 warriors were found awaiting religious instruction. Canada needed missionary priests. Appeals reached Father Oliva just before Christmas. He wrote to Father Nicholas Roger, Marquette's provincial, telling of the need and the necessity to fill the positions at once. His letter concluded: "You have among others Master Marquette whom you can dispatch upon the first occasion." The young theologian, who had been so willing to depend on providence, was summoned from his speculative studies and told to concentrate on moral theology to prepare for the required examination. In the next few months, he passed it. On March 7, 1666, at Toul, he was ordained, and almost immediately he set out for Paris and the port of La Rochelle, from which ships would soon be sailing for New France.

Marquette went to Paris, because the provincial of the French Province of the Jesuits, whose headquarters was in the national capital, was responsible for the Canadian missions. Coming from Champagne Province, Marquette was loaned to this administration for the duration of his work in North America. He would have to see Father Paul Ragueneau, the procurator for the missionaries. Since the latter had been in Canada, consultation with him would be profitable. There were other Jesuit houses on the ordinary route to La Rochelle. One was the college at Orleans on the Loire River. From it Jesuits had gone out to the West Indies, and some had come back. Marquette took advantage of this chance to find out more about mission life. The river flowed westward past La Flèche, where the order had a university. It offered an additional possibility to gain wayside rest and world-wide mission data. That he took advantage of this opportunity is deducible from a letter, still extant, written in 1675 by Father Pierre Cholenec, missionary on the St. Lawrence River at Prairie de la Madeleine. His addressee, Father Jean De Fontenay, had been at Orleans in 1666, when Cholenec was at La Flèche. These two young men both came from Brittany and had never been in the Province of Champagne, but in the letter Cholenec refers to Marquette as a mutual friend. Their only chance to make friends with him was when his packet boat on the Loire tied up at the wharf to let passengers have a look at Orleans and La Flèche. On May 31, 1666, the future missionary of the Mississippi was at La Rochelle and wrote the general in Rome thanking him for the favor he had received in being ordained early and sent to the Canadian mission field. He stated that he had had no preference for going either west or east to work among the infidels until that time. Since obedience had turned him to the land beyond the Atlantic, he had become wholly dedicated to the American Indians and could not wait to be among them.

Marquette did not leave a diary of his ocean crossing. Other Jesuits of his day did. The ships of the period were small wooden sailing vessels. When a fresh breeze swept the sky clean, the sailors broke out the white canvas on mast and spar. The ship became a cloud gliding over a sky of azure water scattering a rain of diamond drops from her bow. Then the calm would come; the sails would hang limp reflected in a salty mirror. The sun beat down. The calking dried and cracked allowing seepage within the hull. Rank odors from this putrid bilge teased the nostrils of the passengers, and they fell sick. Men brought their mats to the deck, but their sleep was broken by feverish groans. Some did not rise in the morning. Weak and delirious, they babbled of their homes and happier times, until their voices trailed away, and they rested in death. The priest, if he was there, wrapped their bodies in a canvas coffin, said a prayer, and the sea claimed its victim. Such calms and perhaps some storms delayed Marquette. It was September 20 when he finally watched the sailors cast anchor in the roadstead beneath Cape Diamond at Quebec.

New France, Louis XIV's colony in North America, was meant to become just that. Talon, the intendant who had been sent to make it such, had the help of Daniel De Remy, Seigneur De Courcelle, as governor. There were three population centers along the St. Lawrence River where they were actively engaged in the transformation. Quebec, divided into the lower city on the banks of the river and the upper city on the promontory something like the rock of Laon, was a strange amalgam of Parisian veneer spread over aboriginal savagery. The governor's château might have taken a place among the dwellings of minor nobility in old France. The Jesuit college and church, the Ursuline convent, and Hôtel Dieu (hospital of the Augustinian nuns) were not unlike substantial buildings of the same sort such as Marquette was accustomed to in Europe. The cathedral was not another Nôtre Dame de Laon, but it would have compared well with St. Pierre le Viel. Bishop François De Laval De Montmorency's home was simple but solid. The citadel was a pile of masonry quite worthy of engineers trained in the school of Vauban, with cannon sticking their noses through its ports. There were a number of large homes in the upper city. The warehouses and shops along the wharfs were in the lower town. For a hamlet of a few hundred inhabitants, it seemed prosperous and urbane; but just upstream, a stone's throw from the harbor, was Sillery. In 1666, it was a Jesuit attempt at an "Indian Reduction"—a village populated by painted savages, who were transplanted there in the hope of

24

Frenchifying them in more peaceful surroundings. At this time, their wild brothers south of the St. Lawrence were on the warpath. When Marquette first put foot on shore, the governor was recruiting volunteers to smash the savage forays of an Iroquois offensive aimed at ending white intrusion into their hunting grounds.

De Courcelle led the attack on the Five Nations while Marquette was still at Quebec. On October 10, the young Jesuit followed the advancing militia for seventy-five miles to the second population center of Canada. Trois Rivières was a typical French provincial parish of 153 souls clustered around their church where Jesuits administered to their spiritual needs. At this time, Governor Pierre Boucher was strengthening his little fortress against the possibility of an Indian raid during the absence of the troops. The church rectory, where Marquette had come to begin a study of the native dialects under the pastor, Father Gabriel Druillettes, was next door to the governor's home.

The last dense settlement, about seventy-five miles further in the interior, was La Ville Ste. Marie, on the island of Montreal, just opposite the Richelieu River. The priests of St. Sulpice were seigniors of this whole island. At Ville Ste. Marie (present-day Montreal), their seminary, a hospital, the church, the fort, and the governor's home were buildings such as might be found in France; only a mile west along the shore, however, were the St. Louis Rapids. Beyond them was the "mystery of the north," a wilderness populated by wild beasts and wild men. On the north side of the island, the Ottawa River spilled its fast stream into the St. Lawrence. It was the route to the tribes which lived *en haut,* "up above" as the Canadians called the territory around *Lac Superieur,* the northern-most of the Great Lakes.

In 1665, Father Claude Allouez had been the first Jesuit to get to the far end of the greatest of the five inland lakes. There he founded a mission among the Ottawa. His account of the great gathering of their tribes had furnished the occasion for Marquette's early ordination. Now the young missionary turned his alert intellect to the mastery of the Algonquin language, which was basic for communication with these people. His success in this brain-teasing, tongue-twisting experiment once more contradicts assertions of those who have pictured him as an indifferent student. In two years, he had mastered six Algonquin and Iroquois dialects.

CHAPTER 4:

TO LAKE SUPERIOR

In 1668, Father François Le Mercier, mission superior, found Marquette ready to begin his active life. In the meantime, the De Tracy-De Courcelle expedition had been successful, The Iroquois, beaten and humbled, had made peace; the route *en haut* was unimpeded. Where the St. Mary's River tumbles down its rapids from Lake Superior to Lake Huron was designated as the field for the new missionary. Here, as early as 1641, Father Isaac Jogues and Father Charles Raymbault had made a visit. They brought back news of a place swarming with Indians attracted there by the good fishing. On April 21, with a *donné*, Brother Louys Le Boême, and a young Indian boy, Marquette set out, paddling a canoe upstream toward the destiny which had attracted him for so many years.

Several biographers of Marquette have yielded to their own imaginations rather than to evidence when they have pictured him as delicate in health and weak in constitution. In reality, he had all the strength necessary to enjoy digging a paddle into the river with strokes which drove him ahead against the current. Father Le Mercier was surprised at his fine physical condition on the first day he came ashore at Quebec from the debilitating sea voyage. The night after he met him, Le Mercier wrote in the college diary: "Father James Marquette arrived in good health in the seventh ship." And now, in 1668, as he sent the young man into the woods, Le Mercier wrote a letter describing him as being of "sound health" and "robust body." The letter containing these words was the annual one to his provincial required by Jesuit rule. Ignatius Loyola had thought of these letters as a means to let the different communities of Jesuits know what was going on throughout the order. The descriptions of happenings in New France so caught the fancy of people in the mother country that, after 1632, they were prepared for publication. Sebastien Cramoisy's press printed the periodical, known thereafter as the Jesuit *Relations*. From 1669 until his death, Marquette's activity is included in this annual; therefore, much about this period of his life has been preserved.

On his way west, the new missionary supplied the baptismal ceremonies for an Indian baby in the chapel of his friend Pierre Boucher, who in 1667 had moved to a seigniory in sight of Montreal where the little Sabrevoix flows into the St. Lawrence. The baptismal register, with the entry in his own script, is still to be seen in the Holy Family Church at Boucherville, Quebec, Canada.

The trip up the rock-banked Ottawa River and into its tributary, the Mattawan, passed forty portages, including the overland pull to Lake Nipissing. Wading through the white water, dragging the canoe, or unloading everything to carry it around a waterfall had left little time for anything else. Now, however, the canoes moved easily along the lake bank and floated out of the French River into Georgian Bay. From there they hugged the north shore, following the channel behind Manitoulin Islands. Here the eye roved over a vast alley of emerald-green water, guarded by a virgin forest of towering pines standing in close array along either side—truly a romantic setting.

It was high summer when the little Indian who was being brought back to his people pointed out the stream that Father Jogues had named St. Mary's River and which came from Lake Superior. A few leagues against the rapid current brought the travelers within earshot of the cascade (*sault* in French) that barred its course. On the southern bank, in an amphitheatre of timberclad hills, a large cluster of Ojibway (French for Chippewa) cabins came into sight. Before the canoe grated on the pebble beach, the youngster was splashing in the water, running to greet his family. The friendly Indians swarmed along the shore to welcome the black-robed priest and his lay helpers. Of course, there had to be councils and presents, and Marquette made his first official speech in Algonquin. Within a few days, a simple chapel and a cell for the priest were erected, and the first city within the present boundaries of the state of Michigan was begun. The present-day Sault Ste. Marie covers the site where, in 1668, Marquette built the primitive white man's home at the foot of the St. Mary's Falls.

From the time, seven years before, when Pierre Esprit Radisson and Médard Chouart Sieur Des Groseilliers had led a flotilla laden with furs from the Straits of Mackinac to Montreal, the Chippewa had been in contact with French traders. They wanted them to come among them with their glass beads, iron tools, tobacco, and "fire water." As a gesture, they gave willing ears to the teaching of Marquette. After a few months among them, he wrote: "It only rests with the missionaries to baptize the entire population to the number of two thousand." However, he wondered if they were not "too acquiescent" and might not "cling to their customary superstitions" after baptism; therefore he continued instructing and encouraging them; but, for the most part, he baptized only the dying, "who are a surer harvest."[1]

Perhaps Louis Jolliet had met Father Marquette in Quebec. In 1666, when the priest passed by, the young Canadian was a seminarian preparing for work in Bishop Laval's diocese. Such young clerics attended the Jesuit college. In the summer of 1669, at Sault Ste. Marie, the two future discoverers of the Mississippi were thrown together for some weeks and probably first conceived the idea of a search for the "Great River." In 1667, with Laval's approval, Louis had made up his mind that the priesthood was not his vocation. He finished his education at the college and went to Europe, probably to delve into the science of cartography. This probability is indicated by his eventual appointment as Royal Hydrographer of New France and the ability in making maps which he demonstrated on various occasions prior to receiving such official recognition. He spent only a year in France. He was back in Canada in 1668 and, with money loaned to him by his friendly bishop, invested in the fur trade. He joined a company that his older brother Adrian and some of his friends were forming with the consent of Talon, who wished to have the elder Jolliet investigate the possibility of an easier east-west route. In the spring the brothers, with four canoes laden for the trade, pushed off from Ville Ste. Marie for *en haut.* On about the first anniversary of Marquette's arrival, some of his Indian neophytes came hurrying to his cabin with shouts of joy to announce that the long-awaited Frenchmen had been seen downstream.

Twelve months had gone by without a word from beyond the horizon of the mission. Marquette could scarcely believe that it had been so long. With many strange, new things demanding his consideration, he had given small thought to the passing of the months.

He had spent weeks tuning his ear to the Indians' guttural utterances. Months elapsed before he was sure that they were beginning to understand the ideas of religion that he wished to impart. Their speech simply did not have words for most of the common concepts of Christianity. Without their having some knowledge of these basic concepts, his efforts to draw them away from superstition and pagan morality had been slow in obtaining any results. His planning and labor for their betterment had been time-consuming and demanding of his full attention. To win the aborigines to his purpose, he had eaten with them, visited their lodges, and cared for their sick. He found that he accomplished more by practicing Christianity among them than by preaching how Christianity should be practiced. Now, suddenly, the anticipation of seeing some of his own countrymen made him aware of the world outside. How pleasant it would be to hear from friends or perhaps to receive a letter from France. He stepped to the door and glanced at the chapel. With Brother Le Boême's skillful carpentry, it had assumed a very neat appearance. He walked to the gate of the palisade that rendered a sense of privacy to the mission compound. There he stood while every Indian in the village lined the river bank, gazing at the four canoes which were approaching. His presence gave assurance of peace. In a few minutes the traders were on dry land.

There was need for some of the *voyageurs* to guard their wares against the too-enthusiastic curiosity of the would-be customers, but Louis and Adrian made their way to the priest. Of course, they were allowed to pack their goods within the staked inclosure. This may have been one of the first examples of what later became a custom. In the wilderness in subsequent years, traders often turned to the one safe place, the attic of the mission church, to store their valuables. Because these often included furs, some misinterpretation has arisen over the place of the missionaries in the trade. The accusation that they were in the trade for a profit was first made by their enemies and later it was repeated by unsuspecting historians. It has been refuted again and again.[2]

Adrian Jolliet was serious about fulfilling his commission. Quickly he put his men to building a cluster of cabins to house them and to serve as the company's headquarters. Meanwhile, with Marquette's help, he made inquiry about the possibility of traveling the west and south sides of Lake Huron in search of an easy passage into Lake Ontario. Since he did not dream how long such an exploration would take, he shoved off to begin it after only a few days at the Sault. Louis was left in charge. How well Adrian succeeded in proving the feasibility of the Great Lakes' route between upper and lower Canada is told by the Sulpician, René De Bréhant De Galinée, who, with a priest companion, François Dollier De Casson, met him a few weeks later near Niagara Falls.[3]

CHAPTER 5:

FIRST THOUGHT OF
AN EXPLORATION

Transient tribes who came to St. Mary's for the summer fishing were curious. They thronged into the office of the new storekeeper, bartering, begging, planning future traffic for the articles of their desire. Fascinated, they sat in the neat chapel, eyes riveted on the simple religious pictures, ears alert for the chaplain's interpretations of what was depicted there. It was only after the long summer day ended and sleep had enfolded the Indian camp that Jolliet and Marquette could sit and talk about the things which Louis had seen in Europe. He had arrived in France at about the time Louis XIV had begun probing the possibility of expanding his kingdom to the Rhine River. Toward this end, French fusiliers had invaded the

Spanish Netherlands on the pretense of protecting the inheritance rights of the Infanta, Louis's wife. Despite the mad Charles, his brother-in-law in the Escorial, and the debonair Charles, his cousin in the palace of St. James, who were ready to join hands with him, there were patriots in Spain and parliamentarians in England who succeeded in raising armies to oppose this French dream. Face to face with this reaction, the French monarch sought respite by the Peace of Aix-la-Chappelle just as Jolliet was leaving for Canada. Parisians understood their monarch's mood. They were sure he would return to complete the operation as soon as an opiate of intrigue had put the patient into narcosis.

The bourgeoisie and commoners with whom Jolliet had mingled abroad knew enough about the merchants of England and Spain to curse the policy of the French court. Both of its imperialistic rivals were blessed with larger fleets than belonged to France. War would give them the opportunity to exploit the resources of the Orient and Occident. English shopmen had chopped off the head of their king, Charles I, when he stood in their way. They had prospered from their takeover of the colonies he held along the Atlantic coast of North America. For almost a century Iberian jobbers had financed the armadas which plied the sea from New Spain to Seville, stuffed with silver, gold, and precious raw materials. Their soldiers of fortune had spread out over much of South America; and they were filling up Central America. These gold-hungry Spaniards were not to be stopped by the lethargy of their half-witted ruler chloroformed by the wiles of his ambitious French neighbor.

Jolliet paused in his appraisal of European affairs. He and Marquette were looking out the window on the richest prize of the New World. How far had the Spaniards pushed north? Would the British, now possessors of Fort Orange, where the Mohawk and Hudson Rivers joined, infiltrate the Iroquois country and then go further on? The two young Frenchmen were silent.

It was Father Marquette's turn to speak. In June, he told Louis, Father Allouez had stopped by while going from the mission of the Holy Spirit at Chequamegon Bay near the far end of Lake Superior to Quebec. In 1666, some visiting Indians who had called themselves Illinois had told him of their home to the south along a river called "Messipi." It was a stream rising in the north at a place where no one had ever been. It swept past their home and off to the south far beyond the longest journeys of their people. It was the Father of Waters because it received the tribute of innumerable streams and bore the booty away to the place from which all water came. Father Allouez thought this meant that the river emptied into the ocean near Virginia. If so, would it not supply a route by which the British might outflank New France? If, instead, "Messipi" went to the Gulf of Mexico or to the South Sea (Pacific Ocean), had the Spaniards

30

reached it already? And how far had they traveled upstream from New Spain? The two young men looked out again on the mystery of this *terra incognita*. Why should they not anticipate disaster by an exploration which would map the Mississippi? Then France would be the possessor of the lands it drained.

The Jolliet brothers had brought no letters from Quebec and for good reason. Father Allouez's visit to Father Le Mercier had persuaded the superior of the Canadian missions that there was need for more men and more organization in the Ottawa country. Thereupon Father Claude Dablon, with the mail for *en haut*, was dispatched to the Sault as lieutenant superior and resident missionary. Father Allouez was to found a new mission among the Potawatomi who were congregated at the base of the *Grande Baye*, less euphemistically known as *Baye des Puants*, Bay of the Stinkers. Today it is Green Bay in Wisconsin, so called by English-speaking settlers who took the French pronunciation of *grande* (that is "gron") to be a mispronunciation of green. Father Marquette was to take over the mission left vacant at the Point of the Holy Spirit, where Allouez had been.

Father Dablon was optimistic by nature, but he was a very practical optimist in execution. As soon as he had heard of the planned exploration, he was very much in favor of it. However, there was no sense in trying to do anything that year. It was already late in the month of August. With Dablon's blessing on an expedition for the next summer, Marquette was encouraged to make all possible preparations for it in the meantime. If he would come to the Sault early in the spring, when the annual mission letter went to Quebec, Le Mercier's lieutenant would add his weight to a request for the trip. If the permission was granted, it could begin in the fall of 1670.

The Ottawa, whose flotilla had brought Dablon, had fished and feasted and were ready to go. In the last week of August, Marquette was manning a paddle in one of their canoes as they crept along the south shore of Lake Superior. August was turning into September and the most beautiful season of the year in this country was at hand. When the birch barks appeared opposite the towering pictured rocks, rising perpendicular to the water, even the savages rested their paddles on their knees and looked with awe while the waves chased by the wind ran to the protection of the shore only to be hustled back by the stonehearted sentinels guarding this solitude. At Keweenaw Bay Father Marquette dreamed of his confrere, Réne Ménard, the first Black Robe missionary of Lake Superior, who in 1662, inland from this place, had fallen victim to the bloody tomahawk of the Sioux. The flotilla turned into the narrow fiord which almost cuts through the Keweenaw Peninsula, made a short portage, and camped at the Ontonagon River to look for bits of copper frequently found there. By then the entire shore of northern

31

Michigan had been skirted. On the 13th of September, while the autumn sunshine filtered through the lace curtains of the clouds to illuminate the lake, the Apostle Islands came into view. This night the missionary kindled a little fire on the hearth of the cabin built by Father Allouez and offered his prayers of thanks in the chapel dedicated to the Holy Spirit of the Point. Here, south and west of the present city of Ashland, Wisconsin, a half dozen permanent villages of various tribes were grouped together. Never had he seen so many Indians, and never had he met such indifference from them.

Chequamegon Bay was the refuge for several savage nations which had fled before the Iroquois. Here were the people of Huronia. From the lands where Brebeuf had given his life for them, they had sought refuge among the Ottawa in the Michilimackinac country where the straits bind Lake Huron to Lake Michigan. Even there the Iroquois pursued them; and they fled again, taking their hosts with them to the remote bay at the west end of Lake Superior. Here Allouez found them. Despair, multiple defeats, and addiction to alcohol had so brutalized the Huron tribes that little of the religious spirit was left in them. Religion had never taken root among the Ottawa. They had lived without a missionary until this time. Now "the Great Captain of the French" (De Courcelle) had driven their foes from the river route which led to Montreal's taverns. For the past few summers they had taken this road to find relief in liquor. These celebrations had almost deprived them of all self-respect. Allouez had small success in rousing such people from their unhallowed stupor. In leaving the Point after four unproductive years, he had told the Indians that he would not return. He shook the dust from his shoes, but the drama failed to touch them. After he was gone, only the fear of their abandonment motivated them to request another priest. This was Marquette's new mission.

When Marquette turned to the Hurons in hope of finding a spark of faith beneath the ashes of their dereliction, he realized that their pagan association had nearly led them to bestiality. Despite the odds, he took up the task of rebuilding their integrity. Guarding his own soul by a reconsecration of himself by vow to God, he went among them. He spoke to them in their own language; he listened to them with a sympathetic ear; he cared for their sick in their wigwams; he brought their dead to his chapel for burial. Such things, coupled with irrepressible good will and prayer, had their effect. By Christmas the former mission Indians had re-established allegiance with the Church.

To do what he did took all of Marquette's waking hours, and his sleeping hours became fewer and fewer. However, the Mississippi often flowed into his dreams. His Indian charges had adopted a young man from the Illinois nation, and Marquette took him for a teacher. Proud of his new dignity, the youth proved an indefatigable preceptor. Marquette's scholarly habits and good memory made him a remarkable student. By Lent of 1670, Marquette had learned much of the new dialect.

CHAPTER 6:

THE TRIP DELAYED

Easter came on the 6th of April in 1670. The sun, just north of the vernal equinox, had little warmth. The winter at Chequamegon Bay had been long and hungry. The Indians talked of the fruitful fishing in the rapids where their lake leaped down into Lake Huron. Running their traps on snowshoes, they had collected enough beaver pelts to make the memory of Montreal's taverns distracting to the strongest of them. The temptation for action turned their heads. They slipped away. Each day the remnant of the tribes at the Point grew less. Shortly after proclaiming the Resurrection, Marquette made up his mind to go with one of the parties traveling to the East. If he were to wait much longer, there might be no way of getting to the Sault, where the possibility of the exploration awaited him.

When he asked passage for himself and his Illinois friend, the extent of his influence on the community may be seen. The elders called a council. They spoke eloquently of their need for him who had restored some sense of dignity to their lives. They revealed their suspicion that he might not come back in the autumn, because they suspected that he was about to depart in search of the father of waters. They feared that he would find a new life work among the people whose language they had watched him learn from the companion he now took with him. Before they granted his request, they asked that he promise to come back in the fall when they would reunite here at the Point. Such a demonstration of good will could not be neglected.

River or no river, he was a missionary. He remembered when he had arrived among them eight months ago. How far they had come since then! How far they had yet to go to be sure of eternal life! He promised them that he would either return or send another father like himself to carry on. This was all they wanted. No more time was wasted: the canoes were ready in the open water of Lake Superior; his few necessities were carried out over the crust of ice which clung to the shore. Before he knew it, he was retracing the trip of last summer, but this voyage was much different. Only the stark skeletons of the birches and maples remained. The pines, partly clad in torn remnants of midwinter ermine, seemed dead, too. Gray clouds spread a somber pall from horizon to horizon. The black water of the lake drove eastward in long billowing swells. After a constant northwest blow, it would create an obstacle field where sharp-edged chunks of ice tossed in crazy patterns to menace the slight siding of birch bark, which alone stood between the fleeing occupants and a watery grave. It took a month to make the trip that had required but a fortnight last September. When he finally arrived at the Sault, Marquette admitted that he had never spent another thirty days in such "constant peril of my life."

Any civilized abode would have been welcome after the trip the priest had made; but when Father Dablon led him to the church on which Brother Le Boême and he had lavished their attention, Marquette knelt in a polished oak pew, looked up at a French madonna in a golden frame, and Notre Dame de Laon did not seem too far away. In the substantial rectory he was assigned to a room with the luxury of a latch on a real door. At evening Jolliet came in. He joined the Jesuits at their table. The conversation soon turned to the Mississippi. If Marquette would write to Father Le Mercier in Quebec about the need of a replacement at the Point of the Holy Spirit, the canoes ready to go *la bas* ("down there") could take the letter to him in time for him to act this summer. When the flotilla returned in September, the exploration of the Great River might begin.

No time was lost: the request was committed to paper, and Father Dablon approved it. As soon as the Indians had gorged themselves on white fish, they had begun to drift away, down the St. Mary's River toward Lake Huron. Before they were all gone Marquette had the message ready for them to take along. In spite of his desire to depart, he paused to reflect on the process of softening which he had sensed among the Huron and Ottawa. A strategic moment had come for the tribes of Chequamegon Bay. It was no time to desert the vineyard just when the grapes were growing ripe. However, the Illinois had so many good qualities, and, he wrote, "Those seen by me are of apparently good disposition." Moreover, he had studied their language with the young Indian from their homeland, which was on "a large river almost a league wide." The tribes "east-southeast" of the Illinois, he had heard, "wear beads, which shows their intercourse with Europeans." He believed that "this great river can hardly empty in Virginia, and we rather believe that its mouth [never yet heard of] is in California." He said that he wished to "go into this river as soon as we can with a Frenchman [Jolliet] and this young man given me, who knows some of these languages." But all this he knew could only be done, "if it please God to send some Father, he will take my place" when the Ottawa and Huron assemble again at the Point; and "I, to execute the orders

34

of our Father Superior [Le Mercier] go and begin the mission to the Illinois." Before the last canoe was out of sight, the petition was on its way.

Perhaps a visit on May 25th from the two Sulpicians, Galinée and De Casson, who had talked with Adrian as he came east by the Great Lakes' route, made Marquette certain that Louis Jolliet would be his partner. The news brought by the *abbés,* who had retraced Adrian's voyage, meant that the latter had discharged his government commission. Surely he would not be long in coming up to the Sault this summer to complete his fur trade business. Louis would then be free to go exploring as a *donné* of the Jesuit, a position which would shield him from all criticism of jealous trappers of the lower St. Lawrence.

Father Dablon was delighted to have Marquette with him. The great influx of Indian fishermen afforded manifold opportunities for unending missionary work. Both priests were kept busy. Jolliet was busy also, because the same influx was his business potential. Most of the summer boarders brought along a certain number of pelts, and his office was thronged with speculators and bargain hunters. As the day approached when Adrian might be expected, Louis was satisfied with the results of his enterprise and knew his older brother could have done no better on his own. Both priest and layman took advantage of their contacts with strange tribesmen to find out more about the river of their ambition. When night brought an end to their toil, they sat for a while and compared notes. Jolliet sketched maps of possible routes that might lead to the Mississippi. Some Mascoutin Indians from the Fox River area told him of Illinois visitors who came down from the west by this stream. Indeed, some of the Mascoutins' more venturesome young men had pushed their canoes to the very source of the Fox. There they had seen signs on the shore of what might have been a portage path to the west. They had not dared to investigate further, because it would lead them in the direction of the Sioux.

Rapidly days turned into weeks. It was past mid-July when, with a wisp of song and a discharge of musketry, the first *coureurs-de-bois* ("free-lance trappers") put in their appearance. They brought excitement, banter, and news. Adrian was not with them, but a staid burgeois would not be expected to travel among these fellows who played the game of life for such high stakes, who moved their pawns so jauntily even when their opponent was death, who were checkmated so frequently. When things quieted down a bit, Louis asked about his brother. Did anyone know his plans? Oh! *Mon Dieu!* Had he not heard? Adrian was dead. They did not know just what had happened, no one had ever seen him after the Sulpicians. An Indian coming to Three Rivers had given such good proof of his death that the notary, Jean Casson, had declared his wife a widow.

By now Le Sieur Beau Soleil might be her second husband. He had not been slow to press his suit. Women were so few in Canada that an eligible young lady would not long remain in mourning.[1]

That night Louis's meeting with Father Marquette assumed a more serious tone than usual. Adrian's death left him the full responsibility for making good to the investors in the company. If something happened to him while on the exploration of the river, who could take over? He had a younger brother, Zacherie, but it was too late to think of getting news to him in time for him to come this year. In addition, Zacherie had no share in the stock of the present company. A new incorporation would be necessary in order for him to come west to ply the trade. Such legal arrangements took time. Perhaps Father Marquette should go alone to the Mississippi with the young Illinois who had taught him their speech. The priest demurred. It was a project that neither could undertake without the other. Jolliet, the trader, had goods that the Indians sought eagerly; Marquette, the missionary, had the message of peace that would free them from pagan fear. Jolliet's maps and Marquette's skill in the language made this an adventure for the two of them, not for either one single-handedly.

No conclusion was reached that night or for several weeks thereafter. Actually, they were still tossing possibilities around when the Ottawa flotilla came back at the end of the summer. Old Father Druillettes was among the Indians, but he was to help at the Sault. He brought word from Father Le Mercier that there was no replacement for Marquette. So it was settled; the Mississippi trip was off. Keeping the promise he had made, one aspiring explorer embarked with his neophytes to continue as their spiritual father in the Mission of the Holy Spirit. The other turned to his traps for another winter. Jacques was already in the canoe when Louis grasped his hand; the priest returned the pressure. The gesture was a pledge not to forget each other when the time came to seek the Great River, which had temporarily flowed out of their lives. The fate of the native Illinois language teacher is never mentioned again. Probably, when he saw how things were going, he took Indian leave and set out alone for places and faces formerly familiar to him.

CHAPTER 7:

TO LAKE MICHIGAN

With the presence of Father Druillettes at St. Mary's, the daily needs of the Indians were adequately met. With Jolliet tied down to the duties of supervising the curing and baling of his furs, the repair of equipment, and the packaging of trade goods for the winter, he hardly left his office. This being the case, Father Dablon, who had taken so great an interest in the quest of the Mississippi, decided to do a little exploring on his own. He had a double excuse for doing so. First, as quasi-superior of the missions in the Northwest, he had a duty to pay a visit of encouragement to Father Allouez. The latter's new work at Green Bay had not left him the time to come north that summer (1670). Secondly, since 1668, Brother Le Boême had worked so steadily building and improving the mission compound that the falls had never been out of earshot for him. Through Jolliet they obtained a canoe.[1] Thus, the priest and the temporal coadjutor began a trip which led not only to Father Allouez (at present-day De Pere, Wisconsin) but also up the Fox River to the home of the Mascoutins, now the city of Berlin in the same state.

Everything went well. Weather, water, country, wild rice, wild fruit, wild fowl—all were so good, all so delighted the optimistic Jesuit that he commandeered the greater part of the *Relation for 1670-1671* to tell about these things. Back at the Sault he set forth so many evidences that the supposed portage at the source of the Fox River led over the height of land to the western-flowing waters and the Mississippi, that Jolliet began transposing to his sketch maps landmarks which the superior had seen or heard of during his travels, indicating the locations and distances from one to the other according to his estimates. Such activity kept his interest keen for the possible discovery. Since his only chance to go exploring depended on a new company with Zacherie as partner, he began to think that he would make a quick trip to Quebec the next summer. He sounded out his hired men. They all agreed that it was worth staying at the Sault if he would promise to take them on the Mississippi trip.[2] In Quebec he knew Bishop Laval. Surely a bishop could exert enough influence on Father Le Mercier to have him send a replacement for Father Marquette and commission him to investigate the Illinois prospects. Since missionaries had always been privileged to go where they wished in the wilderness and were not strictly limited in the number of helpers they took with them, Zacherie could care for the business while his priest friend, his *voyageurs,* and he made a fast dash to the Mississippi. The scheme delayed departure until autumn (1671), but he could think of no other possibility for realizing the adventure Marquette and he had first planned two years before.

There was much coming and going at Sault Ste. Marie every fall just before the first hard freeze of winter. The summer visitors had to get home. Fishermen who had been occupied with other things might dart in for a day or two, hoping to be rewarded with a few kettles of fish. Then they were gone. Dablon, who had no talent for Indian languages, was unable to enter the strange tepees set up by these alien people, here tonight and gone tomorrow. One day as he passed just such a transient settlement, the chief spoke a few words of French to him. Dablon gathered that the speaker had just brought his "long house," his whole clan with uncles, aunts, and cousins, from the Point and wanted to make a home right here for the winter. From the Point—Father Marquette's mission? What was the matter? Druillettes was summoned. They asked the chief, who proved to be a Huron, for the full story.

The Indian's speech was solemn and eloquent. Momentarily, the old priest would interrupt by raising his hand and translating for Dablon. Here is a digest of what he heard: Chequamegon Bay, where the Huron and Ottawa had taken refuge in their flight from the Iroquois, was close to the home of the Sioux, who dominated all the hunting grounds west of Lake Superior. They were the Iroquois of the West, and fear of them had always haunted the mission Indians. Just after Father Marquette and Father Allouez had exchanged places in 1669, a delegation from the Lakota Sioux had come out of the forest with a peace pipe. Largely through the missionary's help, a treaty of friendship had been proclaimed and sanctioned by the exchange of gifts, among which Marquette had included certain holy pictures that had deeply impressed the pagan Sioux. When the mission Indians scattered after Easter, 1670, some of the Ottawa had presumed to take advantage of the ratified covenant to hunt in Sioux territory. They were ambushed and led away as prisoners; about to be tied to the stake, they had invoked the diplomatic accord between their people and their captors. Their juridical plea succeeded. The Lakota chief spared them on their promise of future respect for territorial boundaries. Because some of the young men, deprived of the torture holiday, made threats against the captives, the chief set out with them to assure safe conduct. At a distance considered by them far enough from danger, the protected turned on their protector. While the chief was sleeping, the Ottawa braves plunged a knife into his heart and scalped him. The treacherous Ottawa then hurried to the Point, exulting in their prowess. Such was the sad state of affairs which greeted Father Marquette when he came back to the Mission of the Holy Spirit to keep his promise in the fall of 1670.

The leaves were a riot of ruby and gold when a second delegation from the Lakota came out of the forest. Their faces were daubed black in mourning. Everywhere from the gorgeous autumn foliage other blackened faces peered toward the surprised Ottawa. Beneath each face an arrow waited on a taut bowstring. With exquisite Indian etiquette the ambassadors returned to Father Marquette his gift of small religious pictures. Pivoting in their tracks, with stately mien and in complete silence, they stalked back into the forest. The blackened faces and the arrows disappeared. Through the night the mission Indians shivered in their lodges. It was not the raw air but weak hearts which chilled their blood. On the morning of the following day Dablon's informant and his family had fled. He was sure that the Ottawa would follow. They were no match for such a foe. The speaker wondered whether they could stay at the Sault.

Dablon and Druillettes weighed the matter on the scales of experience while the candle on the rectory table grew shorter and the night wore on. Huron and Ottawa would not mix well with their Chippewa. Manitoulin Islands had been the home of the Ottawa. The Huron had lived near the Straits of Mackinac. The Iroquois were no longer to be feared since De Courcelle had negotiated a treaty with them. It would be best to move the immigrants to locations familiar to some of the older members of each tribe. The Huron chief was told of the decision on the following morning. He accepted the verdict when Dablon volunteered to go with his clan. On the Island of Mackinac the savages felt safe. There a chapel was built as other canoes from Chequamegon Bay began to arrive. The Jesuit received them and stayed with them during the winter.[3]

At the Mission of the Holy Spirit, Father Marquette watched the desertion of one long house after another. The more timid of his flock were fading away, seeking safety nearer the French. But the harvest and the fishing were good this year. With the coming of winter, most of the Indians sensed no immediate danger. Nevertheless, the uncertainty of life had been brought to the attention of the Ottawa in a striking manner. Their first reaction was to inquire about Black Robe's ideas concerning man's destiny after death. Then one tribe among them, the Kiskakon, took the step he had been working for so long. They asked for instruction. They moved close to the chapel so that the winter snow would not hinder them from being present when the missionary wished to teach them about the Great Spirit and initiate them into his language—the prayer. From dawn to darkness, forgetful of all else, Marquette made himself available to guide them toward the faith. Many changed their conduct so completely and asked for baptism so sincerely that the priest could not refuse them. Those who had manifested such unconcern at his first coming now pestered him with manifestations of respect. When they heard that a messenger of God was called an angel, they christened their instructor "Angel of the Ottawa."

One day, about the same time that this providential turn of events was taking place at the Mission of the Holy Spirit, Jolliet glanced through the door of his cabin at the Mission of St. Mary of the Sault and recognized a man approaching with the lumbering, sliding gait of a snowshoe racer. It was Nicholas Perrot. The two had known each other in Quebec; but Louis wondered how he had arrived here at this season. The answer was quick in coming. Jean Talon, the intendant, had sent him as interpreter for Simon François Daumont, Sieur De St. Lusson, who had been commissioned to make sure of three things in the West: first, the allegiance of the Indians; second, the possibility of a route across the continent; and third, the existence of copper mines near Lake Superior. A late start and an early storm had stopped the expedition among some of the friendly Ottawa, who were freshly settled on Manitoulin Islands according to Dablon and Druillettes's plan. There the French had dug in for the winter. Perrot had come on to make sure there would be some Indians at the Sault when De St. Lusson would come to tell them his message from the king. A few days later this intrepid pioneer, who was to be identified with the West as governor at Green Bay, was gone as he had come. By late May the success of his errand was evident. Tribe after tribe was temporarily encamped at the mission. Father Allouez had come from St. François Xavier on the Fox River with the people whose name it bears; and besides the Ottawa and Huron there were Mascoutin, Potawatomi, Winnebago, and Miami mingling with the Chippewa.

On June 4, 1671, announced by musket volleys and shouting *voyageurs,* the ambassador of Louis XIV to the aborigines of America stepped ashore in all the splendor of a blue velvet coat with gold braid and lace at his throat and wrists. A powdered wig was on his head, a plumed hat in one hand, and a gleaming sword in the other. Two flintlock pistols were stuffed in his broad silk sash. He was followed by a squad of soldiers in bright blue-and-white uniforms. Thereafter, for ten days the place resounded with celebration. Presents were brought from the royal canoes. Councils, feasts, dances, and excitement filled the Indians' waking hours. Then, on June 14, came the solemn profession of loyalty. A great cross made from ax-hewn timbers was erected. De St. Lusson threw a piece of sod in the air and read a French act of possession which was signed by all the French and nailed to a tree. The soldiers fired their guns. Father Allouez preached a sermon in Algonquin about the

40

man who suddenly had become king of the Indians. He told them how kingly a man he was. "His house is longer than from here to the head of the Sault"—that is more than half a league—"and higher than the tallest of your trees; . . . our ships in France hold . . . as many as a thousand." The *Te Deum* was sung. Then there was feasting again, until night turned into day on the 15th. Perrot noticed in the morning that the proclamation and arms of France had been stolen during the night; but already the river was speckled with the skiffs of the departing savages. Those who were not on their way were not in a mood to be reasoned with; so he retired for a little rest without perceiving another flotilla of canoes just coming to shore.[4] The first to realize its presence was Father Dablon, when Father Marquette stepped into his room. Had he come, on request, to attend the ceremony? Not at all! He and his Indians were deserting the Point at Chequamegon Bay. To his superior he rendered this account for doing so.

Deep snow covered the stubble in the corn fields. A feathery white carpet spread out beneath the trees. New Year's Day, 1671, was close at hand when the first incident occurred. A young brave ventured into the woods. He was found lifeless, an arrow in his back, a bloody pillow of snow under his scalpless head. What began incidentally soon happened regularly. The dead Lakota chief became a deadly peril to the Algonquin people who were living at the mission. In the dead of winter when ordinarily even the killing bear and the devilish wolf pack were immobilized, death from the Sioux waited just inside the forest of the bay. The Sioux were not waiting for spring before carrying their vengeance to the steps of Marquette's chapel. As the days grew longer their audacity increased. Squaws who went out to plant maize never returned. Men who went to fish among the Apostle Islands disappeared forever. Consternation blazed into a flame of frenzied fear among the pagans. Even the Christians were shaken by the premonition of what might be when so fierce a foe came out of the woods and up from the water intent on overwhelming their villages, burning their lodges, and torturing their folk. While there was yet a chance to avoid disaster, they determined to follow the advance guard, which had fled to the safety of the French in the autumn. Families crowded into their canoes. The torch was set to whatever they could not find room for. Untended, the fire stole through the debris, ignited the bark-covered long houses, and leaped to the roof of the Chapel of the Holy Spirit. Soon a column of smoke was all that remained where the Jesuits had hoped for such great results. Where would Marquette's Indians stop? When he rejoined them, some of the Huron were already on their way to seek relatives who had wintered on Mackinac Island. With them went the Christian Kiskakon. The rest of the Ottawa were heading toward Manitoulin Islands to join those of their tribes who recently had been established there.

Marquette's sorrow over the Indian desertion of the Point became perplexity when they in turn deserted him. What was his responsibility? In the priests' house he found that Father Dablon had the answer. In the comings and goings of the last few days, he had received a letter from the pen of Father Paul Oliva, the Jesuit general in Rome. It told him that the care of the whole Canadian mission was to become his charge. In his new capacity Dablon appointed Marquette missionary to the Hurons. This would take him to a new area in the south. The letter also had a personal message for Marquette. Through it the general had placed the seal of final approval on his priestly work by inviting him to make his perpetual vows as a Jesuit spiritual coadjutor. If Marquette accepted, his enlistment in the Company of Jesus was indissoluble; hence, he should ponder the decision in an eight-day retreat before taking the step. Of course, Marquette was ready to begin the retreat. Before he did so, the Sieur De St. Lusson wished to question him and Jolliet on the possibility of employing the Mississippi as a way across the continent. Dablon had arranged this meeting to help the ambassador solve the second item on the agenda of his western trek.

CHAPTER 8:

MAKING DECISIONS

The two laymen met the two priests in the common room of the rectory. By the time they parted De St. Lusson had decided that he need seek no further for a transcontinental passage until the possibilities of the Mississippi were explored; and he was convinced that Jolliet and Marquette were the men best equipped to explore them. However, he told them that Governor De Courcelle was resigning, that the intendant Talon, whom he represented, had arrived the year before with Franciscan Recollect priests by wish of the king himself, and that rumors in Quebec said the new governor might be a Jansenist. Jansenists hated Jesuits. Perhaps Father Marquette, as one of the order, would not be acceptable as the discoverer of the Mississippi. On this note of uncertainty, the meeting ended. Within a few hours of its termination, the ambassador was off to the Ontonagon River, looking for copper; Jolliet and Father Dablon were on their way to Quebec, the one to take Father

Le Mercier's place, the other to persuade his brother Zacherie to join his fur business in order that someone might take over if De St. Lusson's decision was approved by Talon.

Father Marquette alone remained at the Sault. He had withdrawn himself from the hubbub of the Indian village and was, in the quiet of his cell, following the guidelines set down by St. Ignatius in his book, *The Spiritual Exercises,* while he pondered the divine will in one of the most important decisions of his life. He was making his retreat in preparation for binding himself by the perpetual vows of poverty, chastity, and obedience in the Society of Jesus. On this particular evening the Great River once more flowed into his thoughts. If the authorities in Quebec forbade him to explore it merely because he was a Jesuit, what were to become of all his plans for the conversion of the Illinois, of his long hours devoted to the study of their language? Could he believe that God did not want the faith brought to these noblest of all the aborigines? If he were a diocesan priest under Bishop Laval, the intendant and the governor would not have the prejudice against him which De St. Lusson had mentioned. Would it be better to put off the final vows as a Jesuit and petition his lordship to arrange for a transfer from the authority of Father Dablon to dependence upon the metropolitan of Quebec? As the sun went down, the darkness of desolation filled his soul. However, because God had willed it he had taken his first simple vow of obedience. It was for life. His temptation passed. River or no river, he would not desert the Company of Jesus. He had become a Jesuit with the purpose of going where he was sent, not to try to be sent where he would like to go. On July 2, he placed the document, written and signed in his own script, which made it impossible for him to change his status validly, in the hands of old Father Druillettes. Then he followed the Huron, satisfied to remain with them until death.

In the native tongue, Mackinac meant "turtle." The Island's shape had probably suggested the name. Its sloping shores, which had a circumference of only nine miles, were an inadequate refuge for the many Indians Marquette found there. To the west on the mainland was a high promontory guarding a sheltered bay with prairies and woods behind, which offered everything necessary for a permanent establishment. To this location the missionary shepherded his flock as fast as the transfer could be made. On the bay a new chapel was built with a palisaded Huron village nearby. The Kiskakon set up their lodges a mile to the north. St. Ignace, the name which Dablon had given to the parish on the island, was bestowed on the new mission. Father Marquette was thereby founding a second city in what would become the state of Michigan, the second oldest city in the commonwealth today. Winter was close at hand before these essential things were completed. How busy Marquette must have been with the move is evident from this: for the first time he did not have an opportunity to write the usual letter about the remarkable happenings at his mission for inclusion in the *Relation for 1671-1672.* He must have omitted this duty only because he was too exhausted to keep awake at the end of each day's work.

The episcopal palace in Quebec was substantial but plain. Shortly after his arrival in the capital, Jolliet sought it out. He sat in its study while the affairs which had filled the time between then and now crowded into his mind. This train of events made him wish that his old confidant, Bishop Laval, would not be so slow in coming. He needed the wisdom of his friend to solve the problem created by these things. He had expected to get Zacherie into his fur company and to leave him at the Sault while he went with Father Marquette to investigate the new mission field on the banks of the Mississippi. His younger brother had gladly concurred in this plan; but, when he called on Talon for a patent covering the new business partnership, the intendant had already received the report from Sieur De St. Lusson on his return from the West. It had come just after a letter had been received from Colbert, the minister of the colonies in Paris. This letter explained the imminence of war with Spain and the need to cut off any further Spanish expansion in America. Colbert also ordered that someone be sent at once to carry French occupation to the doors of New Spain.

With De St. Lusson's opinion that the Mississippi was the first route to be investigated as a road across the continent and his approval of Jolliet to do the exploring, Talon found it logical to appoint the young man on sight as official representative of the king and send him forth. To take possession of the river with its tributaries before the Spanish did so would be a wise move. If this move would bring France to the Rio Bravo before Spain crossed it, that would be accomplishing everything the minister wanted. Louis was told that he was to make the exploration. What about Father Marquette and his Illinois mission? The intendant had shrugged off this question. Jolliet must understand that he was being sent for one purpose only—to anticipate all others in carrying the frontier of New France as far as possible by his actual presence on lands not yet seen by any European. To waste no time, he was to go to work at once compiling the lists of necessities for such wayfaring: the number of men and canoes, the required Indian presents and liquor, the food and guns with powder and ball, and the estimated cost of these things and how much the men should receive for wages. Of course, he could have a chaplain; but perhaps he could take a Recollect friar. The Jesuits had enough to do in the missions they had established. With this assertion, the audience terminated abruptly. Jolliet found himself on the street, sure of only one thing—he must quickly have a statement for Talon of the probable expense of saving North

America for France. He realized that Zacherie had not been approved as partner in the trade, and Marquette had not been approved as partner in the exploration. Perhaps the trade could go on alone; but to look for the Great River without Marquette was unthinkable This was the third year they had planned such a voyage together. Marquette was the man who knew the language of the people they would meet. What Marquette had learned from many visiting Illinois had been incorporated on the sketch maps which the priest and he had drawn. He was sure that together they would succeed. He must have Marquette's help.[1]

The door opened, and Monsignor Laval was smiling at his former seminarian. Greetings were mutually cordial. Louis drew a wallet from his belt; with pride in his success, he returned the cash that the bishop had advanced him in 1668 to buy an outfit for the business in which he was then engaged.[2] Then the young man laid his problems on the table. The prelate proved a good listener and did not interrupt until Jolliet was finished. When he spoke, his solution was intelligent and pointed. He himself was so concerned about the secular interference in church affairs that he had decided to go to France to speak with King Louis. However, there was no question that his jurisdiction, perhaps indefinite in power, was most definite in geographical area. The episcopal see of Quebec was coextensive with the farthest borders of New France. Therefore, he would appoint Father Marquette his vicar-general to accompany the expedition and expand the diocese wherever the king's domain should be established. With him in this capacity, no other chaplain would be necessary.[3] As for the budget demands of Talon, the bishop knew the intendant was anxious not to untie the colonial purse strings too often. If Jolliet would propose financing the exploration by a new fur company in which Zacherie was a partner, he believed that a patent would be forthcoming.

The prospectus which Jolliet drew up incorporated the bishop's suggestions. To the intendant the part about the vicar-general, with its assurance of ecclesiastical approbation for state expansion, was gratifying. The proposition for financing the exploration was a very pleasant surprise. Of course, he must not show too much enthusiasm. Also, De Courcelle was still in Quebec. Some governors, when they had left public office, had found excuses for pillaging the profits won by private traders. No such magistrate had ever approved of a new company on the eve of his retirement. Just now dilatory progress was best calculated to advance Jolliet toward the Mississippi. Talon insisted on taking some time to think things over. While he was doing so, the season's first snowstorm spread a white blanket over the Laurentian mountains. When seventeenth-century Canada slipped under winter covers, it went to sleep with the alarm clock set for late in the month of May. Jolliet had to settle down in the city and wait for spring. When, in 1672, the ice broke up in the St. Lawrence River and the first ships from France dropped anchor, they brought the news that war with Spain had probably begun. Actually, the armies of Louis XIV crossed the border of the Spanish Netherlands in August. By then it was known that Louis Buade, Comte De Palluau et De Frontenac, the new governor of Canada, would arrive any day. It was the first week of September before he stepped ashore. The prudent Talon held Jolliet in leash until the new official might approve the steps taken for the Jolliet-Marquette enterprise. At last, on October 2, 1672, with a patent for a new fur company in his pocket and the assurance of both the intendant and the governor that the commission for the exploration included Father Marquette as well as himself, Jolliet began a race with winter to reach the Sault.[4]

It normally took six weeks to go upstream. The Straits of Mackinac are often frozen by early December. In 1672, this was not the case. That year the Jolliet brothers won the race; and in the first week in December Louis paddled the three-day trip to St. Ignace to bring Marquette the news of his appointment. Eighteen months had passed since the two young men had last parted. The priest had found a new joy in his work at a mission where many of the Indians were Christians and all were friendly; yet he had never forgotten the Illinois and their great river. He had frequently commended the matter to the care of the Virgin Mary, Mother of God. The arrival of Louis on December 8, 1672, the feast of her immaculate conception, seemed to him to be a manifestation of her interest. Nevertheless, four years had passed since these two men had first thought of solving the mystery of the Mississippi. What hope could they now have for anticipating Spanish or English explorers? They itched to be off. But, of course, it was foolish to set a date for departure. Louis had to initiate Zacherie into the business at Sault Ste. Marie and make fairly certain of the success of two companies now under his management. The previous year Father Jacques had been prevented from proceeding with the systematic schooling of his neophytes because he had thrown his whole strength and know-how into the essentials of founding a settlement in the wilderness. Trees had to be cleared to make room for corn fields, permanent lodges had to be built and useful belongings had to be transported from the island. He was ever in demand to contribute to the material development of the village and its appurtenances. These activities were still in progress when the annual summer search for food took his congregation abroad. Only a few weeks prior to Jolliet's visit things had begun to be in fairly good order, and an opportunity for the real work of the mission, undistracted by other chores, had opened up. With so much to do before setting out, Marquette and Jolliet spent little time in worrying about what might have happened in the unknown lands to the southwest, or in rejoicing over their commission to go and make an investigation. A few hours after he had come, Jolliet left with a handclasp which meant he would be back as soon as he could in the spring. For the present both men were interested in doing their work, not merely getting it done. Such an attitude makes sand slip through the hourglass rapidly.

CHAPTER 9:

ALL ABOARD

About the first of May Jolliet's trappers were all back at headquarters. Then the native fishermen began arriving. Louis spent a fortnight supervising and advising Zacherie in the methods of dealing with the visitors who brought their winter harvest of pelts with them. At last he was satisfied that things were under control. On May 13, 1673, with his four employees—Pierre Moreau, Jean Plattier, Jean Tiberge, and Jacques Largillier—he said *adieu* to his brother and Father Nouvel, who had succeeded Father Dablon as missionary at St. Mary's. The latter sent a message to Marquette saying that Father Pierson would replace him at St. Ignace. The five men in two canoes glided down the river. Their cargo consisted only of some packages of Indian presents and tobacco, two casks of powder, shot and ball, and the guns of the *voyageurs*. At Marquette's mission they would pick up a few bags of corn and jerked beef. For the rest they would depend on what nature offered them for food and habitation. Thus, when the little flotilla beached in the bay before the chapel of St. Ignace, there was no flurry of preparation. At Mass the next morning, the Indians were told to expect Father Pierson, who would take over the mission while their Black Robe was away. He told them that he expected all of them to care for their prayer house so that it would be in good shape when the new priest arrived. He blessed them and promised to remember them.

One of the two French *donnés* who had been helping Marquette at the mission begged to be made a member of the explorers. He was accepted into their company.[1] The other took charge of the cabin where the missionary lived. The foodstuffs went aboard: the priest tucked a little package of wine and altar breads for saying Mass into the second canoe. Then he picked up his paddle. It was May 17, 1673. As he measured his stroke to that of Jacques Largillier ahead of him, his agile body felt the pleasing vigor of young strength at play. He was only approaching his thirty-sixth birthday, and, with

47

the cassock off for the exercise, his white linen shirt and close-fitting knee trousers revealed a picture of lean, muscular manhood. As the canoes were turning Iroquois Point, he waved to the Indians still strung out along the beach, unable to turn their eyes from "the angel" until he would disappear. How little he dreamed that he would never see this mission again. The soul of this man was to wear out his body in two years and a single day. Before he would come back on May 18, 1675, to die at another site within the limits of the present state of Michigan, he was to journey by the strength of his hands and feet close to four thousand miles through an unmapped wilderness on rivers and aboriginal trails through forests and over prairies. He was to tread the soil from which Wisconsin, Iowa, Missouri, Arkansas, Tennessee, Illinois, and Indiana, as well as Michigan, would grow to become commonwealths of the Union. He was to indicate the overland road by which Americans would occupy two-thirds of their country. Now his attention was concentrated on the rhythm of the paddle beat which the boatmen set to the folk songs they were chanting.

At nightfall on the first day of the trip, the explorers calculated that they had traveled about thirty miles and were well into Lake Michigan. Day after day they skirted the white, sandy beaches framed by hills decked with virgin forest. The weather is likely to be raw in this quarter during the month of May, and rain falls often. If this caused any inconvenience, Marquette's description of the journey overlooks it. He only wrote: "we joyfully Plied our paddles on a portion of Lake huron on That of the Ilinois [Michigan] and into the bay of the Stinkers." The Menominee River is the northernmost river to enter the bay. The expedition turned upstream at its mouth to confer with the Wild Rice tribe. These Indians had known the Jesuits for several years, and Marquette was acquainted with a Christian or two among them. He wanted to see how they were faring. He found them well enough but very solicitous when they heard of his intended trip to the Mississippi. There were startling rumors about the river, including one which located a demon along its banks. It was said that he was a demon whose shouts could be heard "from a great distance, who barred the way, and swallowed up all who ventured to approach him." The priest took pains to scoff at this idea. He did not want them even to repeat the old pagan legends of evil spirits in natural things around them. He stressed the safety of God's protection for those who trust in him and cheerily bade them good-bye.

Coming to the bottom of the bay, Marquette's canoe was given first place, because just up the Fox at the rapids was Allouez's mission center of St. Francis Xavier. The missionary had visited St. Ignace the previous summer, bragging a bit about the architectural gem of a chapel he was building. A promontory was passed, and the little whitewashed structure with a steeple minus a bell came into view. The priest-explorer had hoped to meet his old friend or Father André, who had spent the winter with Allouez. It was too late. There had been no way to send word of the possibility of a visit. Both local men were gone among their Indians. The old man was up the Wolf River at the home of the Fox tribes. André was somewhere along the peninsula between the bay and Lake Michigan which today is picturesque Door County of Wisconsin.

Skirting the shore of Lake Winnebago and Lake Butte des Morts, the explorers kept working up the Fox until, on June 7th, they arrived at the Mascoutin village. Beyond this point, which Allouez called the Mission of St. Mark, the French had not gone. The friendly Indians warmly welcomed the seven white men to their town. They led them to the big cross they had erected in its center. Everyone was in a holiday mood until Jolliet suggested his need of guides to steer his course to the Mississippi. Immediately the Mascoutin became evasive. The Miami, an Illinois tribe who were living with them, wanted no part in a proposed visit to their families. By no means would they think of it; the Sioux country was out there. They had risked their scalps once in getting to St. Mark. The journey was too dangerous to be made twice in a man's life. If their relatives wanted to hear of the Great Spirit, as the Black Robe said they did, let them come and camp here beneath the cross, which was a sign of both divine and French protection. Such a reaction was to be expected, but Jolliet did not give up. He knew Indians loved a council. He displayed some of the European trinkets he had with him and let it be known that these were intended as gifts to accompany words which he wished to speak to them in solemn assembly.

A circle was made. In the center the young trader began his speech emphasizing the principal points by placing a present in full sight of his listeners. Because he knew that some of these braves had been at the Sault two years before when De St. Lusson was there, he recalled all then said about the power of the French king. It was he who wanted the excursion; he would protect the excursionists. The old chiefs demanded a recess to consider these things. At its termination they answered him with savage eloquence. Two days passed in such debates. Finally, Jolliet tried a new tack. He said, above all kings and chiefs of human stature was "the sovereign Master of our lives." No man could stop his decrees. No matter how close the Indians came to the French, no matter how high they built their palisades, if God wished it, they would die. On the other hand, if God wished a man to live, all the Sioux in the world could not kill him. He turned to Father Marquette. Let them look at the Black Robe: without bow or tomahawk he went where they were afraid to go because he had God as his friend. He offered a last present to make them put their trust in God. There was perfect silence as all eyes searched Marquette's face for any sign of disagreement to this testimony of confidence. The image of a man bound to a stake with smoke and fire billowing about him flitted into Marquette's imagination. He realized that this was the kind of death the Indians were wondering whether his God would enable him to undergo without flinching. He knew that he would not bear it alone. But neither did Brebeuf or Lalemant: they had done what they did through their dependence on divine aid. For a moment he became oblivious to the savages. He prayed that he might do what his Jesuit brothers had done if providence required it. He did not notice the quiet departure of the native audience. For a while he and Jolliet stood alone. Then the council reassembled, and it became clear that the priest's faith in God's help had enkindled that faith among its members. They brought "a present consisting of a Mat to serve . . . as a bed during the whole . . . voyage," and two Miami offered their services as guides to the river, if the journey were to begin at once, and if they were not asked to go further than that. It was night. Forty-eight hours had been required for gaining the needed help. In the glow of the campfire Marquette pulled out his writing materials and wrote down what was expected of him as party to this contract. It would be good for him to look at it from time to time. Because he included this reminder in his journal, we become aware of his reflections on this occasion. On the morning of the 10th of June, the French found themselves wending their way up the Fox into a land until then unseen by Europeans.

CHAPTER 10:

THE DISCOVERY

Father Marquette's diary narrates his passage through familiar places from St. Ignace to the Mascoutin village. He tells of experiences familiar to any missionary. Then, suddenly, he was among unfamiliar scenes. He was a trail blazer notching the route by which civilization might cross a continent. The haste or sluggishness of its progress would depend on his ability to set the guide posts clearly for those who would look his way for their direction. His keen observations about what would be useful, his scientific syntheses of the realities he witnessed are as new to his journal as they are time-honored for their wisdom. Here a remedy for serpent stings and a mineral spring are the object of his attention. The wild grapes which festoon the forest may be pressed into wine not only to make glad the heart of man but much more so to make the Mass possible. The trees he names were of all sorts: those proper for house-building, for warming the house when built, for furnishing a table and chairs, and for making chests and bowls. Foods of all sorts are important in his writing. He tells of wild rice and how to harvest it. He catalogs the places where each kind of game abounds and the season when it is most abundant. On the prairie in the early summer he counted the buffalo in a single herd; there were 400. As he went south, he found that two crops of maize were grown in twelve months and that the melons were good, especially the watermelons. He warns, too, of certain hardships to travel, but optimistically suggests remedies which limit their inconvenience. For example, a platform of spaced saplings built high above a smudge fire will protect the sleeper from mosquitoes. Finally, as he went ahead, he kept a compass before him and measured the distance between turns in the stream; thus, he was able to draw for those who would make use of it the most accurate map of the West drawn by any contemporary cartographer.

By the afternoon of June 13, the Fox had become so shallow and so clogged with the lush new growth of water lilies and marsh grass that the men were wading and drawing the canoes. One of the Miami led the way, frequently glancing toward the forest, then riveting his attention on the shore. Suddenly, he froze in his tracks. Jolliet and Marquette came beside him. Without a word, he indicated a depression on the bank; it was the beginning of a weed-grown trace. This was the portage. The Frenchmen motioned to the Indian to go ahead. He neither moved nor spoke. Jolliet reminded him that he had promised to lead them to a river flowing into the Mississippi. The savage gulped. In hurried accents he explained that the river—Marquette thought he called it "the Meskousing"—was very close, just at the end of the path. He and his brother had surely shown faith in the Great Spirit by coming this far. From now on it was foolhardy for so few to venture into a country teeming with Sioux warriors. If the palefaces wished to tempt providence beyond reason, the red men would not. With an impatient sign of farewell, the Indians stealthily began their retreat. In a moment they had disappeared in the rushes.

With loaded guns in reach, some of the men picked up the two canoes. The rest divided the slender bundles of baggage among them. The two explorers led the way. Instinctively, Marquette began counting his paces. Once they were on drier land, the outline of the path became more distinct; it beckoned them on into the foreboding gloom of the forest. The trees on either side extended their protesting arms to stop the intruders. All went forward without a word, tensely alert, walking very cautiously. The priest had counted

51

2500 steps when the woods displayed signs of a fairly recent flood. A hundred paces further small pools stood among the trees. Another hundred and the path faded away in the fresh growth on the bank of a clear stream, its water stained brown by the natural dye of the pine lands through which it had its course. With 2700 steps the French had come from the watershed which drained into the Atlantic to the edge of the Mississippi Valley, through which, they knew, the waters passed either into the Gulf of Mexico or the Pacific Sea. They were determined to find out which one it might be.

With the canoes in what is the Wisconsin River today, Marquette came to a conclusion about thoughts which he had been weighing while he numbered the steps across the height of land. The Miami were right when they said it was foolhardy for seven individuals to go into the hunting ground of all the barbaric aborigines of mid-America if one of them had not been a Black Robe. Because he wore the garb of a missionary, even the Sioux had shown him respect when they went to war with the Ottawa. Responsibility for the whole party weighed on his shoulders. There was only one means for sustaining the burden. At all times Marquette must be the true priest, interested only in the welfare of French and Indian alike. Right now he must convince each of the *voyageurs* to adopt the attitude of his colleagues in the apostolate. While they sat savoring rest and a drag on their pipes, before pushing off on an unknown river gliding into unknown danger, he took a place among them and told them his thoughts. He proposed that they put the rest of the trip under the protection of the Queen of Heaven. The words of a prayer asking her help formed themselves on his lips, and the whole group repeated them after him. Their confidence returned. The men asked that they be reminded daily of their patroness by a repetition of the devotion until the trip was safely completed.

It was high noon on the fourth day after the expedition had started the descent of the Wisconsin. Islands scattered its surface so closely that at times it had been hard to choose the main channel. The forest began where the water ended, and from their canoes the men looked up to shady, windblown caverns in the wall of sun-drenched trees. Highlands could be glimpsed at a distance. As the sun swung westward, the valley narrowed. By mid-afternoon the current of the river, veering to the left, was washing a steep ledge when the two birch barks slid close to its foot. Just ahead a sand bar covered with golden willow saplings shone in bright contrast against a distant, dark bluff which towered 400 feet high and stood at right angles to the course being pursued by the *voyageurs*. Suddenly, the ridge on the left swung away. Jolliet, Marquette, and the men rested their paddles across their knees. The current swept the two birch barks from behind the willow screen. In this instant nature had opened the door to the heart of a continent. Silent in awe, the

52

explorers looked to the right. A vast and placid stream stretched away to the northwest. To the left, between solemn ramparts several miles distant from each other, the Mississippi, Father of Waters, a mile wide at this point, marched majestically toward the sea.

Only Father Marquette has left in writing the reaction of a participant in this singular moment of history. The dream which had begun almost simultaneously with his missionary career was now a reality. The road to the Illinois lay open. If the Great River led to the Pacific, a quarter of the world was about to have its introduction to the faith. Civilization would follow the cross. His vision of families, homes, churches, factories, towns surrounded by farms—a new life for millions of Europe's poor and war-worn people—surpassed all the power of language to express. He wrote simply, "We passed happily into the Missisipi, the 17 june, with a joy which I am unable to make known."

If it was one of those sweet hot days that are frequent in June near the confluence of the Wisconsin and Mississippi Rivers, Marquette and Jolliet would have been tempted to halt for a while. The possible view from the top of the promontory must have pulled at their imaginations. They probably climbed to the summit of the cliff, included in the present Wyalusing State Park. From there a panorama unfolded along the margin of the two stalwart streams in their well-fed valleys, with a hundred tree-covered *coulées* climbing up on either side to the fat fields of the upland prairies. As the sun dipped below the black western escarpment, the river changed into a highway of gold. If Jolliet's journal had not been lost, one could probably have read in it that at this spot he took possession of the Mississippi and the land drained by its tributaries in the name of King Louis XIV of France. The ceremony must have been much simpler (but far more meaningful) than the one that Sieur De St. Lusson had enacted at the Sault.

CHAPTER 11:

THE ILLINOIS

In all the territory the explorers had seen, in all the days of journeying they had made, not an Indian lodge, not a tethered canoe, not a wisp of smoke, not the utterance of a single sound had indicated the presence of human beings other than themselves. Now that they were on the river which led to the towns of the Illinois, the members of the party became particularly alert, hoping to catch a trace of the Indians. On the 25th of June, about 190 miles below the

Wisconsin, the men in the canoe closest to the shore abruptly circled back and landed. They signaled their companions to approach. While waiting, they quietly readied their firearms. When the second birch bark pushed its nose against the bank, its occupants recognized the reason for this behavior. Human footprints on the muddy beach converged on an opening in the rushes; there was also a path. The tracks were fresh enough to make the *voyageurs* certain that those who had made them were close.

The roots of a huge dead tree, deposited on the river strand by some previous flood, offered a stepladder that a man could climb to scan the hinterland. Halfway up, a low exclamation came from the lookout's lips. In the lee of the giant skeleton a backwater had formed. A half dozen clumsy shallops, each hollowed from a single large log, were moored there. Jolliet had used every possible precaution during the descent of the Mississippi. He had even required the party to sleep at anchorage in midstream. Now he posted one man as sentry on the fallen tree. Below him the other four boatmen, loaded guns in hand, were prepared to cover a retreat in case of attack. Speaking quietly enough to hide their presence from lurking savages but loudly enough to be heard by the rest of the party, he and Marquette discussed the situation. The priest knew that the Sioux had come to his old Mission of the Holy Spirit from a neighborhood almost due west of it. Chequamegon Bay was at 46 degrees and 30 minutes north latitude. Each clear night the explorers had turned their astrolabe to the north star to establish their position. The night before, they had calculated that they were at a spot about 40° above the equator. To him it seemed impossible for the Sioux country to extend this far south. He surmised that they had reached the first village of the Illinois. He proposed a friendly approach along the path, quite certain that it would lead to a friendly reception from the Indians. Jolliet's young face was serious. There was logic in what his partner said, but he must make certain that news of the discovery of the Mississippi and of his taking possession of its valley would reach the world. He and Father Marquette would follow the path. The men, under arms and with canoes in the water, were to await their return. If it did not take place within twenty-four hours, they should assume that the worst had happened; with cautious speed they should begin the trip back to Quebec. On arriving there, they should deliver Jolliet's diary to Frontenac and Marquette's to Father Dablon and at the same time account for the absence of their leaders.

The fur trader turned diplomat unstrapped his powder flask, gave his flintlock to one of the men, and turned to Father Marquette, who was pulling on his cassock. The explorers shook hands all around. Perhaps together they said the prayer to the Virgin. Certainly the priest was thinking of his resolution as he stepped in front of

Jolliet and in silence led the way along the narrow, well-trodden path. Maybe he estimated the number of steps taken while saying a decade of his rosary. Somehow he knew that they had been walking for about an hour and a half and had come about six miles when they came to the top of a rise in the prairie and looked down on a cluster of long houses. At a distance, on a small hill, there were two other such groups. Not a soul was in sight; but smoke curled from the vent holes of the lodges, and the smell of cooking fish floated in the air. Evidently the Indians, who had preceded them along the trail, had taken a bountiful catch to the village, and everybody was preparing to eat it. The Frenchmen were so close that they could hear the jabber of conversations punctuated by snatches of laughter. Knowing the Indians' custom to attack with stealth and to announce a friendly visit with loud cries, they spread their hands wide apart and open to signal their being weaponless and let out a shout. Instantly, the occupants of the buildings spilled out pell-mell; almost as quickly they came to a stop when their eyes fell on two empty-handed strangers, one in a long black robe. Then a ceremony was enacted that led Marquette to believe that it had been rehearsed to welcome the coming of the missionary who had been promised to those Illinois who had visited him at Chequamegon Bay.

Four old men slipped over their shoulders the cotton shirts that the French traders had bartered to people of their tribe. They lit pipes and approached with mincing steps, taking an occasional puff of tobacco and offering the smoke to the sun. This was reassuring, and, when the quartet came to a stop without a word, their action was taken as an invitation to speak. In the Illinois language Marquette addressed them with a friendly greeting and asked if they were not of the people whose tongue he used. Delightedly, they replied in the affirmative and held out their pipes for their guests to sample. This formality completed, they led them to one of the cabins. Before the door stood an ancient of the people, his old body uncovered and his eyes lifted toward the sun, which he pretended to regard through the slits between his fingers. Without looking their way, he said, "How beautiful is the sun, O Frenchmen, when you come to visit us; our whole village awaits you, you will go with peace into all our homes." Meanwhile, Marquette observes, "the crowd of people was eating them up with their eyes." Again the calumet was presented. While they were in the act of smoking it, a messenger arrived to tell them that the principal chief awaited them.

With everybody trying to get a better look at them, priest and layman made their way to the abode of the head man. The greeting ceremony was repeated, handshakes were exchanged, another pipe of peace was puffed. Those who could crowded into the structure, surrounding Marquette and Jolliet expectantly; and, because he knew the language, the former made the anticipated speech. As representative of an ambassador of France, his first duty was to make clear the purpose of the present expedition. It was a peaceful exploration intended to go down the river to the sea. Jolliet put a present at the chief's feet to mark approval of this. He repeated the procedure when Marquette paused after announcing his intention of telling all the Indians he met about the God who was their Creator. The missionary once more developed the theme of French regard for the welfare of the natives. For this purpose he dwelt on De Courcelle's punishment of the Iroquois because he knew that they were enemies of the Illinois. Finally, he asked information about the sea to which the Mississippi flowed and the tribes along it to its mouth. Jolliet brought out a third and fourth gift at the proper moment, prompted by a gesture from the speaker.

The chief's response seized on the knowledge of God as what his people wanted most, and he offered a young boy for a hostage to prove his people's good will. The news of peace imposed upon the Iroquois gladdened him. His nation wished nothing more than friendship with all others. A richly decorated calumet was the donation he offered to indicate his sincerity. He ended with an invitation to the Frenchmen to remain with his tribe rather than expose themselves to the dangers further down the Great River. When the missionary tried to explain the lack of fear a Christian has, he found his audience unable to grasp his meaning. Their leader excused their dullness because this was the first contact with Christians they had ever had. He was sure their hungry minds would grow stronger on the missionary's teaching. But now the visitors must be hungry, and he invited them to sit and feast. When the barbaric banquet came to an end, the chief would not hear of his guests leaving in the dark. He made them as comfortable as possible in his own lodge. The next morning, as another sign of lasting friendship, the calumet dance was enacted before Jolliet and Marquette.

The twenty-four hours for visiting were running out. As diplomatically as possible they suggested that the expedition must get under way. Imagine the astonishment of Jolliet and Marquette when they were assured that the Indians would escort them to their boats; and they found themselves retracing their steps along the river path accompanied by about 600 savages. What would be the reaction of the *voyageurs,* after their long and anxious vigil, when they sighted the approach of such a throng of possible enemies? No wonder Marquette tried to keep his black robe visible as the crowd neared the river. Both he and Jolliet moved from group to group, shaking hands in farewell with the hope that their men would recognize in this act the lack of any danger from the friendly mob. Fortunately, it worked. The canoes had stood out from the shore at the first sight and sound of the unexpected procession; but, on seeing their leaders and hearing their voices, the men brought them back to the beach with a stroke or two. The maneuverability of the birch barks evoked exclamations of surprise from the Illinois, who had only their clumsy dugouts as a means of river travel. With a sincere but rapid good-bye to the chief, Jolliet took the lead, Marquette settled down in the second canoe, the orphan Indian boy curled up behind him, and they were happily on their way. The priest noted that it was three o'clock; the visit had almost taken the twenty-four hours allotted for it.

CHAPTER 12:

AN EMPIRE FOR FRANCE

The day spent among the Illinois convinced the explorers that from the Wisconsin to this point they were the first Europeans in the Mississippi Valley. They were dragging the net of French dominion down the mainstream at the rate of about forty miles a day. At each tributary they took possession of all the land watered by the river. Almost a week had passed since they had parted with the hospitable Indians. Their course skirted the eastern shore below a stone-ridged cliff. Some gigantic rocks rose out of the water beside them; and when they rounded one of these, its face bore the image of two fantastic animals so well painted, says Marquette, that "good artists in France would have been pushed to do so well." He could not believe the paintings had come from a savage brush. The two canoes were brought abreast; holding the gunwales, the partners took council. Did the pictures signify that either the English or Spanish had already pre-empted the lands which lay ahead?

Hardly had one apprehension taken shape in the minds of the French pioneers when a more immediate danger presented itself from the opposite shore. A monstrous muddy flood came pouring out between crumbling banks. It caught the drifting shallops and dragged them into the turbulence created by its boiling waters. Decaying vegetation and mouldering driftwood whirled past in weird patterns; whole tree trunks, some naked, others dressed in spring greenery and trailing moss-grown trains of living vines, bore down upon them. It took every bit of human strength and attention to avoid wrecking the canoes. For several miles they were swept along on the crest of this freshet. As soon as the current allowed them to make for the shore, they headed that way. Exhausted, they stepped out on the bank and first realized that their predicament had witnesses. A band of Indians stood in silence about a musket shot from them. Again Marquette threw his cassock about his shoulders and went forward proclaiming friendship in the tongue of the Illinois. Again his greeting was echoed by the elders among the red men, who proved to be of a tribe called Tamaroa.[1]

Once more the white men became the focal point of the friendly eyes of an entire Indian village. Marquette spoke again in solemn council. Following this, the Indians and white men joined in a feast. Finally, there came a time for questions and answers. The representations on the rocks were the work of an Indian medicine man. The Tamaroa knew little of the Mississippi south of them because a demon blocked the way, and hostile enemy nations lived along a stream coming from the east that entered shortly below the demon's lair. Of the turbulent river coming from the west, which they called Pekatanoui [Missouri], they knew a great deal. It flooded at about this time each year. It was always swift and muddy; but in the late summer it afforded a tortuous route to many Indian nations. Far to the west a person could portage from it to a lake draining into a "deep river, which rolled down toward the setting sun and finally plunged into the sea." Marquette spread out his map and the chief indicated about where the homes of the various Indians would be found. The missionary marked these places with a French transliteration of the Indian nomenclature. He compounded the distances estimated between these places. The sum was so great that a conclusion crystallized which had been jelling in his mind. The Mississippi would have had to turn further west long before this if it were to flow into the Pacific. Its constant southerly course meant that its mouth was in the Gulf of Mexico. The Missouri River would be the way by which the North American continent would be crossed. Marquette's mind skipped lightly over the forbidding difficulty of following such a route. He wrote in his journal the newborn hope to be the one who would "proclaim the Gospel to all the nations of this unfledged country who have been sunk so long in the gloom of infidelity."

Relieved by the knowledge that they were the first white men to have come to the mouth of the Missouri, Jolliet added its valley and the valleys of all its tributaries to the lavish donation he was gathering for King Louis. He urged his men ahead with the hope of shaping all of North America into an empire for France. Carried south by muscles so accustomed to the rhythmic tug at the paddles as to flex almost mechanically, and helped by the combined current of two mighty rivers now mingling their strength in one smooth push, the expedition made excellent progress. They were at the confluence with the Ohio River in less than a week. A little way above this spot the mystery of the demon had been solved.

To the west, like a giant standing belly deep in the water, a massive stone tower diverted the rush of the river into a rock-bound cove on the opposite shore. The concave walls received its current, spun it around, and hurled it back upon itself with a roar which the savages imagined to be the cry of an evil genius. This whirlpool had wrecked their boats and drowned their fellows. The Indians portaged around it rather than risking their lives. The two French canoes, approaching with due caution, dashed through the rough tide and in a moment were at ease again on a smooth surface which glided forward with quiet majesty.

At the mouth of the Ohio there were several things which needed consideration; so the expedition went ashore and camped for the night. The mosquitoes made it necessary to kindle a smudge fire. The smudge fire made it necessary to post guards against a possible Indian attack. This precaution led to the first thing which had to be determined. Since the Illinois had advised them that their hunting ground did not go below the whirlpool, what approach should be taken toward strange Indians with whom they could not talk? From here on the aborigines would know nothing about the French. If they were acquainted with European civilization at all, their knowledge came from either the Spanish or the English. One of the Illinois had told Marquette that the Shawnee, who lived on the Ohio, had glass beads. Father Jerome Lalemant, missionary to the Iroquois, had written in the *Relation for 1661-1662* that his Indians, raiding to the southwest, had come upon a beautiful river where the natives had European goods, which he thought were Spanish. Jolliet unwrapped his astrolabe and shot the north star. He determined the latitude as 36° north. They knew that the home of the Iroquois was at about 40° north. This meant that the river they had just passed could flow southwest from the Iroquois village to this point. France was at war with Spain; perhaps barbarian allies of their enemy would attack them at the next village. Perhaps, right now, Spanish troops were advancing up the Mississippi.

Another possibility, a little less unpleasant, was that the English in Virginia, just east of the Iroquois, had advanced into the Mississippi Valley or sent their savage friends to prepare the way. New France was irritated by New England in its back yard, but the two young men had reason to believe that the peace between their king and his cousin on the British throne had been maintained and that the treaty with the Five Nations was still in force. Father Marquette did have a certain proficiency in Huron, a dialect of the Iroquois; hence, after a long night of discussion, the men decided to continue the exploration and to try a friendly greeting in this language on any Indians they might encounter who showed signs of foreign contact. The next morning they went on. Their decision was tested before nightfall.

That afternoon the men had found the current close to the left bank. They were moving along so near to it that they could not see very far inland. Suddenly, some tepees came into view. Whites and Indians saw each other almost simultaneously. The latter reacted naturally to the sudden appearance of strangers. They grasped their arms and took cover. The alarming thing in this movement, however, was that these weapons were not bows and arrows but guns! The confused suppositions of the night before instantly became stark reality demanding instant action. Jolliet ordered a cautious advance toward the shore. Marquette, holding the peace pipe aloft, shouted the prepared salutation in Huron. Distance blurred the words of the reply. He feared the answer was a declaration of war. The *voyageurs* cocked their muskets and moved nearer. Within earshot, the shouts of the gun-carrying savages proved to be entirely unintelligible, but the evident terror evoked by the French could not be mistaken. The braves called their women, who hurried from behind the camp with peace offerings of food. The men dropped their weapons and waded out to help bring the visiting canoes to land. Buffalo meat, bear oil gravy, and white plums were ready for the travelers. Optimistically, Marquette says that the plums were good. By their primitive sign language, the Indians were able to make known that they were on a journey, and that their guns, their knives, all their metal ware and cotton cloth were purchased from white men who had homes far to the east, who had rosaries like Marquette's, who had among them men dressed in robes like his, and who had statues and musical instruments in their lodges. This evidently meant that they traded with the Spanish missions in Florida. But Marquette concluded that these visits to the whites must have been casual indeed, since the visitors had no notion of Christianity. Had the Spanish come to live among them, even briefly, they ought to manifest some signs of religion. He took pains to instruct them in a few basic doctrines and to tie some French-inscribed medals around their necks in order that future meetings with Europeans would reveal their dependence on His Most Christian Majesty, Louis XIV.

Of course, the explorers attempted to ascertain from the people of this aboriginal tourist group how long it would take to travel down the Mississippi to the sea. Their answer in gesticulations was understood to mean that the ocean might be reached in only ten days. Thus encouraged, the French went on, once more assured that European competitors were still far from the Mississippi and that they might place the escutcheon of France at the mouth of the Great River within a few days.

CHAPTER 13:

PRUDENCE PREVAILS

Despite taking his regular shifts at paddling and despite the various adventures since they had entered the Mississippi, Father Marquette kept up his scientific study of the valley's resources. Some of the things already mentioned were seen in the days of July. It was the fifteenth of this month when his concern with these matters was rudely interrupted by an episode which had all the appearance of bringing the whole exploration to a sudden and catastrophic close. The tangle of cottonwood, elm, and linden fringing the river opened up into a considerable clearing filled with well-built, bark-covered long houses of large proportions, each capable of sheltering many families. A cry from a lookout was taken up on all sides. Young warriors armed with bow and arrows, war clubs, and shields swarmed toward the river. Some piled into the great wooden dugouts and commenced an encirclement of the two little birch barks. Others came to a stop at the water's edge, holding their weapons in reserve. The advance guard plunged into the stream with the intention of boarding. Fortunately the current proved too strong and they had to make their way back for shore under cover of drawn bowstrings. Had the seven Frenchmen begun fighting, they would have been overwhelmed quickly.

Father Marquette called to the *voyageurs* to trust their lives to their patroness, the Mother of God, and not to touch their guns, while he kept waving the calumet. Before the arrows were released, two ancients stepped from the crowd. At a sign from them, silence fell over the whooping savages, and bows were allowed to unbend. These elderly leaders waded into the water until it reached their armpits. Holding bow and quiver high in one hand, they beckoned the white men to come toward them with the other. Encouraged by this gesture of good will, the French approached them "with plenty of anxiety." At arm's length from them, the Indians tossed their weapons at the feet of Marquette and Jolliet. Then, while the boatmen brought their barks up into the current, the Indians carefully eased their bodies into the canoes with an agility which seemed incredible in men of their years. Immediately, Father Marquette, still holding the calumet over his head, did his best to express the white men's desire for peace. He pronounced their good will in each of the six languages that he knew. When this elicited no hint of understanding, he signaled to the old men to speak. Their words were completely alien to his ear. The priest, despite his proficiency, admits "at first [he] could not begin to pronounce a few [of their] words, no matter what effort [he] made."

At the bank, with the Indians now jostling each other in their curiosity to see the strangers, Marquette ran over his repertory of greetings again and was happy to hear an old man answer his words in the Illinois vernacular. The elder proved unskilled in this idiom; but, together with what he knew and a lavish utilization of signs, Marquette depended on him as interpreter for a speech which was made to the assembled people. His narrative does not elaborate on the content of his speech. Probably he did not think it worth saving for history, since, as he says, he doubted whether he made his listeners understand anything about the religious section of his address, though he tried his best to be both clear and emphatic. If they missed this religious message, it is probable that they missed the sense of the rest of his remarks. Meanwhile, his auditors kept clear of any formal response. They simply let the French know that their tribal name was "Mitchigamea"; on the next day they would take them to the principal town of their nation, which was called "Akansea." There the chiefs would tell them all they wished to know. Boiled corn meal flavored with fish was portioned out for their supper. Apparently they received no invitation to share the questionable comforts which the long houses offered. With the mosquitoes affording an excuse for lighting a fire, they pulled their canoes within its glow so that they might keep watch over them and be in reach of their loaded guns. By turns they sought individual naps, while anxiety over their situation made it easy for the sentinels to keep awake.

The Indians slept little during the hours of darkness, for they were highly excited about opening this new era in their lives. The wiser elders among them had apparently gathered enough from Marquette's speech to appreciate one aspect that tied in with the arrival of white men at their village—it brought European trade knocking at their door. From the elders the mandate was passed from house to house: it was for their universal good to respect the visitors. Once the Indians had arrived at this decision, messengers were sent at once, dark though it was, to all the tribes of their Quapaw nation to advise them of the good fortune that had come down the Great River in two tiny skiffs such as they had never seen before. The next day Marquette and Jolliet were to learn why it was so important for these aborigines to establish a commercial relationship with the French.

The sunrise on the sixteenth of July was hidden by a gray fog. However, there was light enough to see the way, and the French sought the river at once. The old interpreter was persuaded to enter the second canoe. Offshore, a Mitchigamea convoy awaited them in one of their scows hewn from a giant tree. The crew made signs to follow their lead and started downstream at a steady clip. Hour after hour guide and guided went ahead, until the sun had drawn back the curtain of mist. It was between ten and eleven o'clock when they neared the mouth of the present-day Arkansas River. There they sighted two log shallops approaching with solemnity. Their escort turned around, joined them, and all three approached in single file. A chief in the bow of the foremost shallop began a chant, "quite pleasing to the ear," while body and arms moved gently to the rhythm as he held up a smoking calumet. His crew deftly maneuvered into position so that they were within arm's reach just as the two groups came abreast. The natives held out hands of welcome which Jolliet and Marquette grasped. Instantly, the peace pipe was presented, followed by the peace offering of food, both corn mush and corn bread. By breaking their fast here on the river, friendship was proclaimed. The flotilla then veered into the current and proceeded a half league further down, where a large gathering of lodges came into view. Along the shore, curiously silent, was a great gathering of Indians.

The visitors were helped ashore, and Marquette was delighted to be greeted by a young man "who understood Illinois much better than the interpreter" they had brought along. Falling back, the silent watchers opened a path which led to an arbor neatly carpeted with reed matting. There sat the chief of the warriors and his ancient counselors. Marquette and Jolliet took their places beside them, while everybody from the town now surrounded this new focus of attention. Jolliet placed a present before the head man. Dependent on the Illinois interpreter for his means of communication, Marquette made the speech which the Indians were awaiting. With better help this time, he succeeded in making a simple declaration of the Gospel and the power of prayer. With each point accentuated by a new gift from his partner, he asked two questions: What did the Quapaw know about the sea? Who had furnished the guns to the people who had been met near the Ohio? He ended on the theme that peace among the Indians would assure both friendship and trade goods from France.

The response came easily. The chiefs admired the word about the Great Spirit, and they would appreciate hearing more. The trip to the sea ordinarily was said to require ten days by such transportation as they had. The light birch barks of their visitors might make it in half the time. They went on to say that they had never made the trip because the very Indians who had met the explorers with guns "prevented them from coming to know the Europeans and from having any commerce with them." The hatchets, knives, and glass beads that they had obtained were procured with great difficulty through entrepreneurs who refused to sell them guns. It was down the Mississippi where the Indians with guns lived; and they killed any of the Quapaw who sought to go to the home of the white men to purchase the medicine sticks that, with bits of thunder and lightning, killed from afar. Surely the French had been sent by some good spirit to bring them what they needed to assert their rights. For this they begged them not to risk their lives among the treacherous people downstream, but to bring them some guns so that they could clear the way through the land of the enemy to the sea. During this time a feast was being served. Marquette enjoyed the corn on the cob and watermelon, but he was not enthusiastic about the dog meat. This was the only kind of meat served because the Quapaws' enemies with guns prevented them from ranging afield where there were buffalo.

When the speeches were finished, the crowd took over to make this a happy holiday. They queued up to get a look at their new friends while the squaws served the throng food on earthenware platters. Toward evening Jolliet and Marquette became aware of the almost total absence of men in the still-celebrating crowd. A messenger from the chief arrived and conveyed them to one of the largest lodges, where they soon learned what had occasioned this coincidence. The male population, young and old, jammed the place. In an opening sat the chief and the interpreter. The explorers were ushered to a mat beside them. There they were advised that this council had been called because some of the braves were so anxious for guns that they had proposed murdering the whites and taking the half dozen muskets belonging to them rather than waiting to secure those which traders might bring later. However, common sense had prevailed. The vote had gone against such treachery, said the speaker, and to give "a mark of perfect assurance, he now executed the calumet dance" before Jolliet and Marquette; and, to dispel all fear, he presented his pipe for the missionary to smoke.

With the council ceremonies finished, Marquette and Jolliet pretended to rest on one of the platforms built to catch any stir of air and to foil attacks from mosquitoes. Far from being asleep, they were, as the missionary says in his journal, having "another council, to weigh what we should do, if we should push on further, or whether we should satisfy ourselves with the discovery which we had made." Because of the smog below and the shifting clouds above, Jolliet was not able to measure accurately the angle of the north star. From recent observations he knew that they were lower on the river than 34° north latitude. The young men had placed the southernmost boundary of the English colonies on about this meridian; hence, they surmised that the banks of the Mississippi, which still pursued its way to the south, could not have been settled by Anglo-Saxons. Unaware of its great delta, they thought that the river's mouth was where on the maps they had a deep estuary appeared midway along the north shore of the Gulf of Mexico. In general, according to these maps, this shore lay on a line between the thirtieth and thirty-first parallel north. Estimating a degree at about eighty miles, they decided that the Quapaw were about right in saying that they might get there in five or six days. The discrepancy by which the tourist Indians had indicated about the same length of travel from the Ohio to the sea as the Quapaw now gave for its distance from their village, they attributed to a misunderstanding of their signs. Their intent must have been to indicate the distance from their home below Akansea. The traveling savages were allies of the Spaniards. They had said that they went east to buy their goods; but, with a war to urge them on, might not the Spanish have come west by now to occupy the mouth of the Mississippi? If the French went on, what were the possibilities of seeing salt water and returning safely? The explorers felt lucky to have anticipated all Europeans in taking possession of the valley to this low latitude. If they could speed trade to the Quapaw, they would establish a barrier against foreign intrusion toward the interior of the North American continent, which they had won for France. If they were foolhardy and went too far, thus falling into the hands of the enemy, the news of their success would perish with their capture. With this accomplished, the Spanish would surely hurry upstream. They would take possession of the land and publish the fact to a world unaware of what Marquette and Jolliet had done. Their trip would have been in vain. The layman believed that the all-important thing to do now was to get settlers into the valley, not to settle geographical curiosity about the mouth of its Great River. The missionary felt that the most pressing necessity was to fulfill his promise both to bring the Gospel to the Illinois and to bring other priests for the conversion of the Quapaw. All the possibilities were discussed while the Indians slept. The missionary and the explorer concluded that they had done what they were sent to do: to gain the heart of the continent and to determine the route which led through it. Tomorrow they would start home to avoid the possibility of their success dying with them in a Spanish dungeon.

CHAPTER 14:

REPORTING THE DISCOVERY

Exhausted, the explorers slept. A tropical sun was burning down on them when they woke. The village had awakened before them, but some of the ancients would not allow them to be disturbed. In a ceremonial visit to the chief, Marquette and Jolliet announced that they had decided to accept his advice not to proceed further toward the sea. They promised to encourage French traders to bring European commerce to his people. To impress the people of Akansea that they feared neither treachery from them nor bullets from their enemies, the party of explorers departed in a leisurely manner and according to savage etiquette. They rested and received visitors most of the day. From their almost depleted stores of merchandise, they gave small gifts to those persons who seemed influential. Toward the middle of the afternoon, the two canoes were put into the water. A salute of musketry was fired, sending squaws and children screaming into their lodges and causing admiration among the warriors. Taking advantage of the moment, they dipped their paddles and were off. They began to struggle with all their might against the current as they aimed the birch barks toward Quebec, 2500 miles away. The date was July 17, 1673.

Muscles that had flexed so easily while the explorers journeyed south with the current of the stream now pulled almost to the breaking point in their effort to drag the canoes back in the opposite direction. Twice the work and twice the time were expended in regaining the village of the Mitchigamea. Such exertion could not go on continuously. At shorter and shorter intervals the men came to land and sprawled on the ground, limp with fatigue. At the end of the day they anchored a canoe in the river to fish for food rather than take the few steps needed to seek the buffalo, whose bellowing reached their ears from beyond the canebrake barrier which fringed the stream. The sum of their weaknesses added up to fewer miles covered each day. No wonder Father Marquette did not care to say more about this part of the adventure than what he summarized in fourteen words: "We go up the Mississippi again, taking a beating as we stem its current."

In 1920, in the Duke of Portland's library, Clarence Alvord chanced on a Latin letter dated August 4, 1675, from the "Flumen Convectionis" and signed "Jacobus Macput." It was on a single page

66

of paper certified as a seventeenth-century rewrite of the original which had been received by Colonel Bird of Virginia in the winter of 1675. Knowing that Father Marquette had named the Mississippi "The Conception," the finder hoped that he had come on a letter in which the transcriber had misspelled this word and the priest's name and misinterpreted the date.[1] Those anxious to fill in the blank space from July 17 to August 25 in the missionary's account seized on the document as genuine Marquettiana. Recent research has produced more plausible evidence for tracing it to another Jesuit who wrote from the Connecticut River during King Philip's War, which was in progress in 1675.[2] Therefore, its contents add nothing to the narrative which comes from Marquette's journal. On the fortieth day after leaving Akansea, this journal has the first specific comment about events of the return. On this day, in the neighborhood of the 38° of north latitude, the explorers deserted the Mississippi in favor of another river which they traveled "toward the lake of the Illinois [Lake Michigan] with less punishment."

The date for beginning the new route is not in the text of any manuscript, but it may be deduced from a custom of French explorers to name geographical discoveries after the saint on whose feast day they were found. St. Louis, king of France, has his feast day on August 25, and his name is the one Jolliet used most frequently in speaking of the stream now known as the Illinois River. Some years later he told a Canadian friend, Claude Charles Le Roy De Bacqueville De La Potherie, that his reason for entering its mouth was a word from the little Indian boy, who vouched for its being a shorter road to Lake Michigan.[3] The youngster knew what he was talking about. The Illinois proved broad, deep, and "peaceful." If Father Marquette's sanguine spirit had been unable to effervesce while he bent an aching back over his paddle on the Mississippi, now it bubbled over. "We have not seen anything like this river for richness of the countryside: prairies, woods, buffalo, stags, roe, wild cat, plover, geese, ducks, parroquets and of course beaver. . . ." Progressing through this Eden, they came upon the large Illinois village of Kaskaskia, where he wrote down the name of a tribe—"Peouarea"—which as Peoria became the major city of the valley.

From the valley of the Illinois River came those Indians who had visited Marquette at the Point. They made him renew his promise to return and dwell with them. A chief and his young men accompanied them to the present Des Plaines River, up it, across Mud Lake to the south branch of the Chicago River, and to its mouth in Lake Michigan. By the end of September the seven men who had carried French domain into the Mississippi Valley were at St. Francis Xavier Mission on Green Bay, where they had scarcely paused on the outward trek "about the commencement of June."

Just before Marquette had left Kaskaskia, the Indians had brought him a dying infant, whom he baptized. This was the only occasion on which he had administered this sacrament during the exploration. It is the only thing he mentions as making the trip worthwhile. However, he knew that there was much that he must record both for the benefit of the French Catholics who supported the missionaries and expected to be told how their alms were helping the work in New France, and for his confreres, who would, he hoped, soon be founding missions up and down the Mississippi and its tributaries. The information he had gathered on the location of tribes, on the routes leading to them, on food available, on timber resources, on medicinal plants—all of this would prove most helpful to those destined to come this way. As winter closed in, he had time to organize his field notes. From them he wrote two copies of a journal which he hoped to forward to his superior in the spring.

Jolliet hastened on to the Sault in order to be with Zacherie for the winter of fur trading. He, too, had accounts to write for the officials who had commissioned the expedition. He must draw a map with the latitude and longitude of the realm that Louis XIV might call his own because a Frenchman had preceded all other Europeans in getting there. He must rehearse the ceremonies by which he had taken possession of this landfall. He must detail the best sites for settlements that alone would enable France to hold this empire. He must particularize the economic advantages that would lure the settlers. With so much to do, the daylight hours of the winter were too short, and he was glad when spring came. By the time some Potawatomi arrived from Green Bay with a copy of Marquette's journal for Father Dablon in Quebec, he had finished his own. He locked these papers and some ledgers related to his business in a strong box, stored this carefully in a canoe, and set out with two men and the little Illinois boy, eager to spread the word by which France would know she was welcome in the valley of the Mississippi. Perhaps he was too eager; for, with confidence in his ability to handle the birch bark, he often guided it into the white water along the Ottawa River, exulting in the added speed with which such rapids sent him toward his goal. Thus, he shot the little shell into the last rough place, the Sault St. Louis, almost in sight of Montreal. There the unforeseen happened. In a blinding second Jolliet found himself struggling in the water. A rock was in reach; he grasped it and clung there. Downstream the canoe, bottom up, danced for a moment on the waves, and broke into splinters. He never saw his strong box, his companions, or the little Indian again. As these things disappeared, his own strength seemed to fail. Then he remembered the devotion with which he had undertaken the expedition. With prayers on his lips, he held onto the rock for almost four hours. Finally, a couple of fishermen plucked him from death before he succumbed to exhaustion. He credited his rescue to the Mother of God. As soon as he could, he made his way to Quebec to assure Frontenac of the exploration's success and to tell him that he had left a duplicate of his journal "with the fathers at Sault Ste. Marie."

In the West there were also disasters during the summer of 1674. At St. Mary's Mission ambassadors from those Sioux who had driven the Huron and Ottawa from the Point came to make a treaty of peace. A council met. Some of the local Indians were suspicious of the embassy. Suspicion turned into threats, threats into a brawl, the brawl into a bloody fight to the death. In the course of the slaughter, the mission residence was set on fire. It burned to the ground, consuming the second copy of Jolliet's journal.[4] Fortunately, Father Marquette at Green Bay had kept the second copy of the diary he had sent to Father Dablon. In the autumn he received the latter's request for this document, and he sent it. Since Marquette's is the only remaining journal of the expedition, more is known of its missionary aspect than of its political trappings.

CHAPTER 15:

THE LAST MISSION

The messengers who brought Dablon's request for the duplicate journal were two *donnés* from the mission at the Sault—Pierre Porteret and Jacques Largillier. The latter had been on the expedition. Both were assigned to accompany Father Marquette in laying the foundation of a mission at Kaskaskia. Jacques Largillier could hardly believe that the priest who was so glad to see him again was the same robust athlete who had been able to keep pace with the best of the boatmen on the whole extent of the 1673 exploration. The handshake of greeting was quick, but the fingers which gave it were scrawny. The voice of recognition had been softened by suffering. The body, on which the cassock hung as if draped on a clothes rack, had lost its lithe muscular agility. Only the smile and the spirit were Marquette's. Winter food on the Indian mission was always a mystery that missionaries had found well not to investigate too closely. The sudden change from outdoor life to working with pen and paper may have weakened his resistance. Early in the summer sickness had struck him; a virus of some sort had laid him low. He fell so close to the magnetic field which draws men's souls beyond the grave that his soul almost yielded to the pull; but the crisis had passed, and slowly he had regained enough strength to walk around a little. Now he convinced himself, with more zeal than prudence, that he was strong enough to make the trip south to Kaskaskia.

Several days after the permission came, Pierre, Jacques, and Father Marquette were sitting at a council fire in the Potawatomi village at the mouth of the Fox River. Some Illinois visitors had invited them to be present because they were discussing the pros and cons of accompanying the Black Robe on his trip to their homeland. At so late a day in the autumn the missionary would have wished to be promptly on his way; but Indian etiquette demanded his lending attention to the debate, which terminated after forty-eight hours with the announcement of the Indians' determination to go along. It was the 29th of October, 1674, when the flotilla finally issued from the Fox and coasted into Sturgeon Bay, where the portage to Lake Michigan was begun. Two killing days were spent in dragging canoes and cargo from the Green Bay shore to the shore of Lake Michigan. Then, on November 1, the flotilla turned south and camped at night where the present city of Kewaunee has grown. Because their Indian escort often turned into little streams, seeking hidden swamps and lakes where the migrating water fowl might be surprised, there were few days when they made good progress. It was November 23 when they entered the Milwaukee River. Snow fell that night. Father Marquette experienced fresh symptoms of his illness; but the hunting was so good in the vast marshes just inside the mouth of the stream that the party spent four days in a camp—close to the present area where Kilbourn Avenue crosses the river—before the Illinois could be persuaded to move on.[1]

It was December 4 when they reached the mouth of the Chicago River. The ice on the stream was six inches thick. More snow fell. The Illinois, now in familiar territory, hurried ahead to let their people know that Marquette was on his way.

Pierre and Jacques now took things into their own hands. Up the river about two leagues near the beginning of the portage to Mud Lake, a ravine offered shelter from the north wind. The neighborhood gave evidence of plentiful wild life, which meant the possibility of a food supply. Here they built a cabin and told the priest they were spending the winter on that spot. He accepted the inevitable. On December 8, 1674, the cabin was so far from finished that the water needed in the celebration of Mass could not be kept from freezing. This prevented Marquette from offering the Holy Sacrifice on the feast of the Immaculate Conception. By the ninth the chimney was set and a fire was kindled on the hearth. After that he said Mass daily.

Christmas was near. For almost two weeks Pierre and Jacques had been away. They were searching for some Indians who might be willing to barter a bit of corn from their ever-meager supply. If winter dumped enough snow on the Chicago River camp, a bag of meal might mean the difference between starvation and life. At a distance of about fifty miles they found "La Taupine" and a physician busily trapping beaver. La Taupine was the nickname for Pierre Moreau, who had been one of Jolliet's men on the 1673 trip. Frontenac had taken a fancy to him, so he could engage in the trade without fear. His companion's name remains anonymous, probably because he did not enjoy equal patronage. Moreau obtained some flour for them. The men also persuaded the doctor to come and have a look at their sick friend. He made the trip with the Indian who brought the grain. His intentions were good, but his ministrations did nothing to improve Marquette's condition.

During the December days and nights, while his companions had been on their errand, Marquette had found the situation ideal for making his annual retreat. The rest of his life can only be understood in the light of what happened to him during the silent communing with God. It was at Green Bay on his return from the voyage with Jolliet when such an opportunity had last been his. It had come just after four months of vigorous activity, when his muscles were hard and his body in superb condition; hence, his meditations then had been shot through with brave plans for carrying the faith to the natives in the regions of the Mississippi and the Missouri, perhaps even to the shore of the Pacific Ocean. True, the love of man was only the second great commandment. First came the love of God; therefore, he had renewed the offering of himself to the Lord according to the resolution made one night, in a former retreat, at the Sault. God had taken him at his word and accepted his offering in a supernatural way. Today, twelve months later, he was no longer strong; but still he was ready, like a true lover, to give not only his strength but his life. The boy who at Reims had asked how Brebeuf could be happy in suffering was now suffering himself. But because he had learned Brebeuf's secret, he was happy.

When the doctor left, it snowed. After that the two *donnés* stayed close to the cabin. They suggested a novena for the recovery of Marquette's health. He cooperated and, at the end, told them that he thought he noticed an improvement. He was so cheerful that they hoped it was so. Each evening the three men sat around their hearth. Sometimes, if the day had been trying, the priest spoke, unfolding the mystery of pain in the practice of love. He always listened to his companions remark about travel conditions, food supply, and other important matters that might be helpful to missionaries who would follow his trail. These points he jotted down in his journal and was able to say that, despite his illness, "nothing was lacking to us by way of food . . . we have also lived very comfortably." A less optimistic individual would probably have translated this as, "we had monotonous food, but enough to keep soul and body together . . . and we never were in danger of freezing to death."

On March 28, 1675, when Pierre came into the cabin with a hunting bag of game, he brought news which had been awaited for the last few days. The ice had broken on the Des Plaines River and was on the move. It would soon be free for navigation. The end of the delay was in sight. He would have another look tomorrow. It was pitch-dark in the cabin except for a few glowing coals on the grate. How long the three men had slept is uncertain because, as they awoke, they were distracted from everything else by a strange sound of moving water. They had never heard a murmur from the Chicago River before, though it was just a few feet from their cabin. Only this week the equinoctial sun and a warm south wind had opened holes in its now spongy ice. Now it took only a few steps beyond the threshold to find that it had become a different stream since sunset. From the direction of Mud Lake a flood was tumbling through the ravine where they had wintered. Its surface was rising rapidly. Even while they were sleepily trying to rationalize the situation, the first trickles of water reached into their open door. A big bag of corn meal, their bedding on the floor, moccasins and garments would soon suffer unless quick action was taken. Throwing on all the clothing each one could find, they began evacuating. Everything movable was dragged up the hillside. Guns and powder horns had to be hung on trees with care. Foodstuffs, too, were balanced on branches to keep them dry. Doing this on banks still frozen beneath a bit of slippery mud or snow was slow work. The gray streaks of dawn were welcome. With the uncertain light before sunrise, the salvaging was finished and inventory taken. They had saved everything worthwhile.

The canoe was in good shape. The frail cabin was now surrounded by a torrent which buffeted its walls with the imminent threat of destruction. The deluge came from a new channel that high water in Mud Lake had opened. This probably meant that they could make the passage to the Des Plaines without dragging their skiff and without packing their supplies. These observations were made while they breakfasted as best they could. The *donnés* explored westward, while Father Marquette kept an eye on the equipment. To him the river seemed to sink a bit during the day, but toward evening it rose again; and the explorers returned after witnessing the actuality of their surmise—a water route was open the entire distance between the two streams. The night of the 29th all slept on the hill. On March 30, the shack was still uninhabitable. There seemed no advantage in waiting here any longer. They piled their belongings into the birch bark and dragged it to the placid sloughs threading the island-scattered pond. There they boarded it and pushed ahead. By late morning they were safe on the west shore of the Des Plaines River above an ice jam which had raised the surface of the freshet twelve feet above its normal level and had caused the flood. Father Marquette recognized the spot as the same one from which he and Jolliet had portaged east eighteen months before.

Because of the uncertain conditions below the barricade and a strong south wind whipping spray into the explorers' faces, they set up camp where they were until the ice would go out and the river would return to its ordinary level. This date is not clear from Father Marquette's journal, which has only one more entry. Evidently, to preserve every ounce of strength for what had to be done, he discontinued writing in his daybook. Under the last date, April 6, he wrote once more for those who might come after him. He calls attention to the advantage of travel early in the spring, because then the migrating flocks of "plover, geese, ducks, cranes and other game" frequent the lagoons of the river. Incidentally, he mentions meeting the fur-trapping physician, who thereupon made up his mind to return with the priest and witness the founding of the first permanent mission in Illinois. We can believe that the man dedicated to curing bodies had a professional compulsion to remain with the man dedicated to curing souls, whose body was now so weak. Father Dablon had to depend on Pierre and Jacques for the closing chapter of the missionary's career, up to and including the day of his death. They told a story of his activity at Kaskaskia which is hard to believe possible for a dying man. But that is what he was.[2]

The boatmen's memory for dates was not very exact. Between Monday, April 8, and Wednesday, April 10, the priest was welcomed by the Indians "as an angel from heaven." The Illinois had built him a dwelling similar to the one which had been seen by those who visited him at Chequamegon Bay. They took his baggage to it. Without resting, he started a tour of the long houses to let everyone know he was ready to teach them the prayer. Of course, the chief must receive the first official call. It was the last week of Lent. With the assistance of the head man, Marquette planned to inaugurate the mission on Holy Thursday.

On a prairie bordering the town, poles were set in a circle to make a sort of leaf-covered bower. In the center a silk-draped pylon, at some height above the altar, displayed four pictures of the Blessed Virgin, one facing each point of the compass. Mats and bearskins were arranged all around this center of attraction. When the expected hour came, 500 chiefs and elders sat down in concentric rings close to it. Immediately behind, 1500 young warriors crouched around them. Further out, as many women as possible joined the group. Some brought babies in their arms, others held the hands of children. Some had to be on the move to maintain a semblance of order among the rest of the youngsters who were not old enough to sit quietly but curious enough to run from place to place in search of a better view of what was going on.

The Apostles' Creed is a summary of Christian belief. Father Marquette divided it into ten parts for his sermon. According to Indian custom, each one was introduced by his *donnés,* who moved among the chiefs and offered them small gifts—a thimbleful of beads, a medal, a twist of tobacco. Mindful of the impression Brebeuf's courageous suffering had made upon the Iroquois, Marquette dwelt especially upon the crucifixion of Christ, since it was the "very eve of the great day on which he died on the cross for them as well as for the rest of the world." Finally, he celebrated Mass and gave Communion to the Frenchmen. The congregation was dismissed to ponder the message and return on Easter Sunday, three days later (April 14), if they wished to confirm their desire for the continuation of the mission.

Little time was allotted for eating and sleeping during the next forty-eight hours. Outside Marquette's cabin, the chiefs solemnly waited their turn to propose their questions. Inside they were won by the considerate kindness and willing attention with which each query was received and answered.

Very early on Easter morning all were back at the site of the field Mass. There the Illinois orators brought the reply of the tribe to the missionary. "He had been heard with joy and universal approbation by everyone of the nation." Father Marquette then "celebrated the holy mysteries for a second time . . . and took possession of this Country in the name of Jesus Christ and gave the mission the name of the Immaculate Conception of the Blessed Virgin." Moving away from the altar, his step faltered. Filled with the happiness of an accomplished task, his strength finally ran out. By night he lay prostrate on his pallet with the shadow of death upon him. Unwilling to have any gloom dim the Indians' gladness, he decided that he must not die among them. The next day a procession of anxious visitors crowded through his sickroom to ask about the effect of his health on the new understanding of life which they had hoped he was to teach them. Somehow he found strength to answer each new inquiry with the repeated promise that, despite the need for him to leave now, "either he or another of our Fathers would return to continue this Mission."

On a buffalo robe stretched taut by young warriors, they bore Marquette to his canoe and lowered his disabled body into the center section. To make it easier for Pierre and Jacques to progress upstream, the few pieces of personal baggage which remained were relayed to the Des Plaines River by runners who vied with each other for the honor of doing this service. Only when they had launched the priest's bark on the Chicago River, with the current befriending the paddlers on their way to Lake Michigan, did the young Indians return these packs to their owners. With final solicitude in expediting Marquette's homeward journey, the disconsolate Illinois told him that he would find the beaches more hospitable and the distance to Michilimackinac shorter by coasting along the east shore of their great lake; hence, the boatmen turned south from the mouth of the stream to begin their race with death, knowing they had a slim chance of victory.

CHAPTER 16:

COME HOME

The once powerful frame of the priest was now so feeble and spent that he could not move without the help of his companions; yet, it was he who consoled them in their evident sorrow. He promised that he would watch over their welfare once he was in heaven. With his head propped up on one of the struts between the gunwales, he watched the passing shore, commenting about it. He would close his eyes, and they knew he was praying, because a fervent word or two would escape his lips: "I believe that my Redeemer lives," or "Mary, Mother of grace, Mother of God, remember me." Up to the last day of his life he recited his breviary. As he grew weaker, his joy seemed to increase. He was experiencing the happiness of giving himself to the leader he loved. In this spirit and in a perfectly unconcerned manner, he told Pierre and Jacques how to bury his body and asked them to raise a cross above the grave.

Friday, May 17, Father Marquette contentedly announced as the eve of his departure from this life. On the following day his eyes fell upon a stream washing the foot of a little hill just before losing itself in Lake Michigan. He asked his friends to turn in there because it would be the place where he would die. They did not wish to believe it and acted as if they would go further because the day was "not far advanced." The priest said nothing, but the *donnés* somehow lost their eagerness to go ahead. They turned back and landed where he had said they should. They carried their friend to the shade of the hill where, as they later admitted, with sadness which numbed their sense of what to do, they lit a small fire and put together a bit of a shelter made of branches and bark. They were brought back to reality by the father's voice. He was thanking them cheerily for all they had done for him during the voyage. He asked their pardon for being such a nuisance and promised they would be in the hands of providence for the rest of the trip, since he would remember them as he had said. He offered and they accepted a chance to receive his final absolution. He asked them to take a note to Father Dablon in which he had written his own faults since his last confession. He told his friends to get a little sleep and said he would awaken them when his hour was near.

From where he lay he looked out over a charming little lake that the river had made before its final mingling with the water of the great sea beyond. Shortly before, he had written, "I try to keep ready." Now he was. He offered the same gift in the same spirit as St. Jean De Brebeuf had given it; only the circumstances were different. It made him so happy that he almost forgot to call Pierre and Jacques. Then he heard their voices pronouncing the Holy Name. He repeated it. When a moonbeam glinted on his crucifix, he knew they were holding it for him to see; he had requested them to do so when he was dying. His two friends heard him say the names of Jesus and Mary, then, "all at once he raised his eyes above the cross holding them fixed upon something he seemed to gaze upon with delight, and thus, his face smiling and radiant, he expired without a shudder and with the ease of one falling asleep."

Instinctively, the *donnés* looked skyward toward the constellation of the Great Dipper. By its march around the north star boatmen were accustomed to judge the hours after dark. It was almost midnight on Saturday, May 18, 1675. Had Father Marquette lived thirteen more days, he would have celebrated his thirty-eighth birthday. Intent on time-taking, Pierre and Jacques may not have glimpsed a glowing meteor which actually slipped across the arch of heaven that night. The men knelt silently for a while, then wrapped themselves in their blankets and lay beside his body. At dawn they "put this holy deposit in the place and according to the manner which he had requested of them; and planted there, at the foot, a large cross to serve as a marker to those coming that way."

Father Nouvel, superior at St. Ignace; Father Pierson, who had taken over the mission in 1673 when the exploration left; Pierre and Jacques, the Christian Indians, and the white trappers stood on the beach of East Moran Bay, facing the Island of Mackinac. It was June 7, 1677, the Monday after the feast of Pentecost. The straits were calm, and from the southeast a sedate procession of thirty canoes was approaching. Without the usual cries of welcome, the Kiskakon tribe, returning from the winter hunt, came toward shore soberly and with measured paddle stroke. They had been the first of the Ottawa to yield to Marquette's teaching; and now the reason for their solemnity was their regard for him. Traveling north along the east shore of Lake Michigan, they had been on the alert for the cross that the boatmen had placed there to mark his grave for passers-by.

76

When they had sighted it, they had stopped in the stream by the hill with the pretty lake beyond and had uncovered their missionary's remains. They had found his body incorrupt but, "according to what they customarily do for those whom they hold in high regard," they had separated the bones from the flesh, cleansed them with care, and arranged them "in a box of birch-bark" to bring them home and bury them close to the place where they lived. They had sent ahead to announce what they were bringing, and thus the congregation was waiting on the beach.

The silence was unbroken until the funeral cortege was in earshot of a spoken word from land. At a sign from Father Nouvel, the canoes slowed to a stop before touching the shore. The superior asked about the river, the hill, the lake, the cross which had stood above the grave "to verify that it was truly the body of the Father, which they were bringing." Satisfied with the answers, all tongues once more were quiet, except the one in the chapel bell. It rang out two quivering, silvery notes, listened until they lost themselves across the straits, then sang again. It did this for the time it takes to say the *De profundis* (Psalm 129, "Out of the depths"). "After that the body was carried to the church, with the accompaniment of everything which the ritual requires in such ceremonies." The next day, says Father Dablon, with "full funeral rites, it was placed in a little vault in the center of the church, where he remains as the angel guardian of our Missions for the Ottawa."

The man who established the two oldest towns in Michigan, who with Jolliet first opened the Mississippi Valley to Europeans, who with his partner first trod the beaches of the great river where Wisconsin, Iowa, Illinois, Missouri, Tennessee and Arkansas now are, had returned to the present state of Michigan to die and be buried there. On September 3, 1877, two hundred years later, archaeologists uncovered his grave. They found the church floor, the vault, and only a few of his bones. The rest had been removed by the Indian admirers. The recovered fragments are carefully guarded at Marquette University in Milwaukee, where they remind each new generation of students of a man who discovered that in spending his life doing good to others, he was happiest himself.

NOTES

CHAPTER 1:

1 Reuben G. Thwaites, ed., *The Jesuit Relations and Allied Documents, Travels and Explorations of the Jesuit Missionaries in New France, 1610-1791* (73 vols., Cleveland, 1896-1901), 59:206-207. Thwaites' *Jesuit Relations,* as it will hereinafter be cited, is a reprint of a great many pertinent seventeenth- and eighteenth-century primary sources. Vols. 50 to 60 contain accounts concerned with Marquette.

2 Thwaites, *Jesuit Relations,* 71:400-403, reproduces the only portrait which seems to be a likeness of Marquette. It was made when he was an older man, but has the features mentioned in the text. The evidence for Marquette's good physical development appears in Jesuit domestic documents in the Archivum Romanum Societatis Jesu, hereinafter cited as ARSJ, and is in the collection, Franc. 14:126 and 14:285.

CHAPTER 2:

1 Gilbert J. Garraghan, "Some Newly Discovered Marquette and La Salle Letters," *Archivum Historicum Societatis Jesu,* 4(1935): 268-290.

CHAPTER 4:

1 Thwaites, *Jesuit Relations,* 52:213.

2 Patrick J. Lomasney, "The Canadian Jesuits and the Fur Trade," *Mid-America,* 15(1933):139-150.

3 Jean Delanglez, "Louis Jolliet, Early Years, 1645-1674," *Mid-America,* 27(1945):9-15.

CHAPTER 6:

1 Jean Delanglez, *The Life and Voyages of Louis Jolliet, 1645-1700* (Chicago, 1948), 11-12.

CHAPTER 7:

1 The Chicago Historical Society Archives, *Otto Schmidt Collection,* 2:267, contains the original bill for the canoe. Other originals are available in this depository, in the *Charles Gunther Memorial Collection,* and in the general manuscript collection by consulting its index under "Jolliet."

2 The Archives of the Province of France of the Society of Jesus. *Fonds Brotier,* 166, No. 4:26. Here, one of these men, Jacques Largillier, is said to have made the trip. If he went, it seems sure the others did.

3 Raphael N. Hamilton, "Location of the Mission of St. Ignace from 1670 to 1673," *Michigan History,* 42(1958): 260-266.

4 [Nicolas Perrot], *Memoire sur les Moeurs, Coustumes et Religion des Sauvages de l'Amerique Septentrionale par Nicolas Perrot* (J[ules] Tailhan, ed., Leipzig-Paris, 1864), 128.

CHAPTER 8:

1 Arch. Prov. Franc., *Fonds Brotier*, 155:11, sets forth Jolliet's wish to have Marquette with him, in a contemporary document.

2 Amedée Gosselin, "Jean Jolliet et Ses Enfants," *Proceedings and Transactions of the Royal Society of Canada,* 14(s.3, sec.1):71.

3 John G. Shea, *The History of the Catholic Church in the United States* (4 vols., New York, 1886-1892), 1:313 and n.1.

4 Delanglez, "Jolliet, Early Years," *Mid-America,* 27:22 and n.78.

CHAPTER 9:

1 ARSJ, *Franc.* 23:301 and *Franc.* 23:320.

CHAPTER 12:

1 Jean Delanglez, "Tonti Letters," *Mid-America,* 21(1939):238, transcribes a letter which establishes this visit. The original is in the Archives of the Seminary, Quebec, *Missions,* No. 49.

CHAPTER 14:

1 Clarence W. Alvord, "An Unrecognized Father Marquette Letter," *American Historical Review,* 25(1919-1920): 676-680.

2 Raphael N. Hamilton, unprinted manuscript, Marquette University Archives, HM, Series 3, Box 5, B, "Marquette's Place in History," 279.

3 Claude C.-Le R. De Bacqueville De La Potherie, *Voyage de l'Amerique* (4 vols., Paris, 1722), 2:131.

4 Raphael N. Hamilton, *Marquette's Explorations: The Narratives Re-examined* (Madison, Wis., 1970), Ch. 4, is a consideration of problems related to the discovery.

CHAPTER 15:

1 Raphael N. Hamilton, "Father Marquette's Visit to Milwaukee," *Historical Messenger of the Milwaukee County Historical Society,* 23(1967):44-47.

2 Arch. Prov. Franc., *Fonds Brotier,* 166, No. 4:26.

BIBLIOGRAPHICAL ESSAY

For more information about the country and society which Father Marquette knew while he was a missionary and explorer in North America, one should probably begin with some of the more general histories of the French colony. An interesting narrative of this sort is John A. Caruso, *The Mississippi Valley Frontier* (Indianapolis, 1966). It has a bibliography of many standard works and is intimately related to the scene of the 1673 discovery. There is a volume in the *Chronicles of Canada Series,* Thomas G. Marquis, *The Jesuit Missions* (Toronto, 1916), which deals with many of the men of the order who were active in New France. Francis Parkman's series, *France and England in North America,* has been reprinted many times. It is the classic description of the imperialistic struggle of these powers. His *Jesuits in North America in the Seventeenth Century* and *La Salle and the Discovery of the Great West* make exciting reading.

Nothing will give the true feel of missionary work among the Indians like reading the original letters. R. G. Thwaites, *Jesuit Relations and Allied Documents,* was reprinted in 1959 and should be in all college and university libraries. Marquette's own descriptions of his work are found in volumes fifty to sixty. For some of the most interesting details of his life, the student must turn to periodical literature. *Mid-America,* published by Loyola University, Chicago, Illinois, has many scholarly articles by Jean Delanglez, who also wrote *Life and Voyages of Louis Jolliet* (Chicago, 1948), just a year before his death. *Michigan History,* in its volumes for 1958, 1964, 1965 and 1968, has printed accounts related to Father Marquette. Finally, for a longer, more detailed account of Marquette's life students may consult Joseph P. Donnelly's *Jacques Marquette* (Chicago, 1968); or the present author's *Marquette's Explorations: The Narratives Reexamined* (Madison, 1970), in which significant facts from widely separated sources have been brought together.

DATE DUE